Great-Looking 2x4 Furniture

Stevie Henderson
with Mark Baldwin

Great-Looking 2x4 Furniture

Stevie Henderson
with Mark Baldwin

Sterling Publishing Co., Inc.   New York
A Sterling/Lark Book

Editor: Chris Rich
Art Director: Kathy Holmes
Photography: Evan Bracken
Production: Elaine Thompson
Illustrations: Orrin Lundgren

Library of Congress Cataloging-in-Publication Data Available

A Sterling/Lark Book

10 9 8 7 6 5 4 3 2 1

Published by Sterling Publishing Co., Inc.
387 Park Avenue South, New York, NY 10016

Created and produced by Altamont Press, Inc.
50 College Street, Asheville, NC 28801

© 1996 by Stevie Henderson
Distributed in Canada by Sterling Publishing
C/o Canadian Manda Group, One Atlantic Avenue, Suite 105
Toronto, Ontario, Canada M6K 3E7

Distributed in Great Britain by Chrysalis Books
64 Brewery Road, London N7 9NT, England

Distributed in Australia by Capricorn Link (Australia) Pty. Ltd.
P.O. Box 704, Windsor, NSW 2756, Australia

Printed in Hong Kong
All rights reserved

Sterling ISBN 1-4027-0780-0

CONTENTS

This book is dedicated to twelve remarkable women, each of whom has made an immense difference in my life. One I have known for over fifty years; some are new friends. They are (in alphabetical order):

Ellen Mahoney Biondolillo

Cheri Cetto

Patrice Connolly

Sandra Fisher

Patti Kertz

Barbara McMahon-Ritzhaupt

Anita Miller

Linda Milstead

Jackie Nelson

Virginia Newby

Diane Thompson

Bette Wood-Hall

Although each of these women is unique, they all share some of the same wonderful traits. Their courage has inspired me, their accomplishments have astounded me, their minds have challenged me, their hearts have nurtured me, their humor has cheered me, their common sense has guided me, and their compassion has consoled me.

The world is a better place because these women exist. I am grateful to call them my friends.

Stevie Henderson

INTRODUCTION

This book was written with one clear goal in mind: to give readers who have longed to try their hand at woodworking a way to jump right in. If you think that woodworking is a mysterious pastime practiced only by kindly, gray-haired men with leather tool aprons and fifty years' practice, you're about to discover that you're wrong. Master woodworkers aren't the sole keepers of the flame. If you can imagine yourself cutting a board, hammering nails, and driving screws, you can work with wood. Although you probably won't be capable of making reproductions of Chippendale chairs in the first two weeks, you certainly will be able to construct good-looking, sturdy, and useful furniture for your home. That's what this book is about.

The projects in *Great-Looking 2 x 4 Furniture*, which range from incredibly simple to slightly more complex, are designed to eliminate the need for advanced woodworking skills. Many of them also take advantage of pre-made materials now available to the do-it-yourselfer—materials that make it easier to have fun while you learn. Why drive yourself crazy with complex wood-joinery techniques to make a cabinet door, when shutter doors are available at building-supply stores? Or worry about turning a table leg on a lathe when you can add a purchased finial to the end of a 4 x 4 instead? Woodworking—especially when you're first starting out—should be a pleasure, not a stress-inducing puzzle.

You've never used a saw before? Start by reading the first section, "Tips and Techniques," where you'll find descriptions of basic tools and how to use them, advice on purchasing lumber and supplies, and important safety tips. Then select a simple project; all the projects in this book are keyed to indicate the skill levels required to make them. With the help of step-by-step instructions, detailed illustrations, and complete lists of required materials and supplies, you'll soon be standing back to admire your finished handiwork.

If you're an advanced woodworker with a workshop full of high-powered and high-priced stationary tools, don't despair. You, too, can make these projects! You may need to modify the instructions to accommodate your tools and knowledge, but this won't be difficult to do.

As experts already know, the best aspect of "doing-it-yourself" isn't just producing high-quality products for a very low price. It's the sense of accomplishment that making them yourself brings. Developing your skills won't take fifty years of practice, either. Why? Because woodworking skills and enthusiasm tend to build themselves. The more you work with wood, the more eager (and able) you'll be to tackle increasingly challenging projects and to enjoy the increasingly significant rewards.

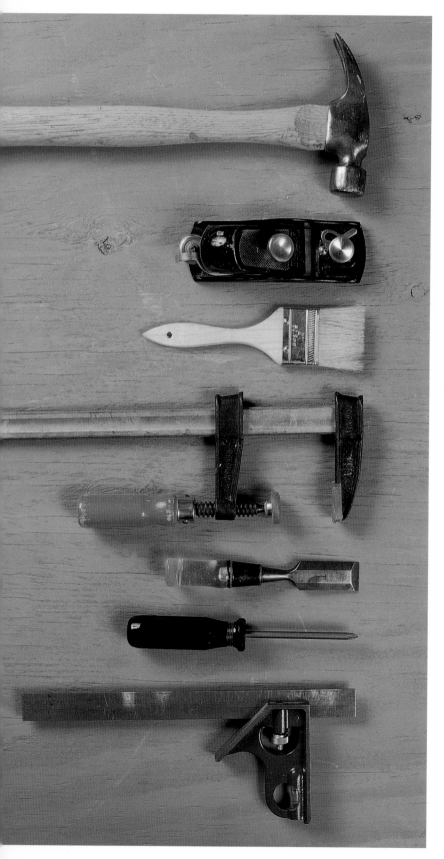

Tips and Techniques

Like every craft, woodworking has its own language and its own set of specialized tools, but rest assured. Learning to speak the language and use the tools is several thousand times easier than going to medical school or studying nuclear fission. Once in a rare while, of course, you'll run into an employee at a building-supply store or lumberyard who'd like to make you believe you're too young, too old, too stupid, or the wrong gender to practice "his" craft. Ignore folks like these, and head for the hundreds of others who haven't forgotten that they started out where you probably are now. You'll discover that most woodworkers who know their stuff are a remarkably helpful, humble, and friendly lot.

Read this section carefully. You won't find every answer to every question, but you will find the information you'll need to build your first several projects. By the time you've finished reading it, you'll be calling a circular saw a circular saw instead of "one of those electric cutting things with a blade that goes round and round," and you won't feel cheated when the 2 x 4s that you buy turn out to be 1-1/2" thick and 3-1/2" wide.

Tools

Woodworking tools are generally divided into three categories: hand tools such as hammers, screwdrivers, and hand saws; portable power tools, including circular saws and electric drills; and stationary power tools such as table saws and band saws.

Any wood project can be constructed with hand tools alone. Because many fine woodworkers enjoy the process as much as the result, they never use anything electrical. Power tools aren't necessary to produce high-quality results, but they do the work a lot faster. My goal is completing projects quickly (preferably before my weekend guests arrive), so over the years I've added power tools because they save time and physical effort. Today, I use a power drill rather than a screwdriver and a table saw rather than a hand saw. I started out with hand tools and built up my collection by adding a tool to my workshop each time I constructed a large project. Even with the expense of these purchases, however, I spent less money than I would have if I'd purchased ready-made furniture.

Always buy the best tools you can afford. This advice applies to all tools, not just to stationary power tools. A poorly made hammer can be just as frustrating to use as a poorly made table saw. You may find a cut-rate set of screwdrivers, but they won't seem like such a bargain when the plastic handles break off the first time you use them. Read the warranty, too. If the manufacturer offers a lifetime guarantee, the tools are probably top-notch.

The projects in this book require some basic tools that you may own already and that will make useful additions to your household if you don't. Some tools, such as a saw and a set of screwdrivers, are needed for every project, but others, such as a staple gun, are only required for a few pieces. You may want to choose your first project to match the tools you have available. Start by reading through the project instructions to determine which tools you'll need.

Consider your physical size and ability when you purchase your tools. A golf club or a tennis racquet must be matched to the person using it. In the same way, large hammers work best when large people are using them. Lifting a large hammer again and again would wear me out. I'm more comfortable with a lighter one, even though I have to strike a nail more times to drive it in. The same philosophy applies to power tools. A great deal of strength is required to control a large belt sander, so I prefer using a less powerful orbital or finishing sander.

BASIC TOOLS

—A smooth and level working surface

—An assortment of flathead and Phillips screwdrivers in different sizes

—One large and one small claw hammer and a tack hammer

—A nail set

—Two wooden hand clamps and two "C" clamps

—A tape measure, straightedge, level, and combination square

—Hand saws (a combination saw or rip saw and crosscut saw)

—A hand-operated or power drill and a variety of bits

—A sanding block and an assortment of sandpaper from fine to coarse

—Goggles and a dust mask

OPTIONAL TOOLS

—Two bar clamps, two pipe clamps, and a web clamp

—A framing square and sliding T-bevel

—A circular saw and a selection of blades, a plane, a saber saw, and chisels in 1/4", 3/4", and 1" widths

—A staple gun

—An orbital or finishing sander

ADVANCED TOOLS

—A table saw and a band saw

—A belt sander

—A router

Working Surface

Probably the single most important tool in woodworking is a smooth and level work surface. If you're working on an uneven garage floor, you won't be able to determine whether the legs on the table you're building are square and even. The work surface doesn't have to be great to look at; it just has to be level and even. An old door (flush, not paneled) or a piece of thick plywood supported by sawhorses will work just as well as a professional-quality workbench.

Whatever surface you choose, also make certain that it's large enough to accommodate the project you're building, that its surface is smooth, and that it's solid enough not to shift as you work. (For instructions on leveling, see "Measuring Tools" on the opposite page.)

Hammers

You'll need a couple of hammers (large and small) for the obvious nailing jobs. You'll also find that a tack hammer, for driving in small wire brads and tacks, comes in handy. A nail set (see page 20) will help you countersink nail heads so that they sit below the surface of the wood.

Clamps

A variety of clamps is essential for woodworking. You'll use them not only to apply pressure and hold joints together until the glue sets, but also as valuable aids when assembling your projects. By using clamps, a single person can assemble even a large project—a job that would otherwise require the concerted effort of several people.

Get two clamps of each type you buy; you'll almost always use them in pairs to provide even pressure. Wooden hand clamps should be your first choice if you're just starting your tool collection. They're extremely versatile, as they can be adjusted to clamp offsetting surfaces.

When you apply clamps, always insert a piece of wood or a commercial clamp pad between the clamp and your work. Without this cushion, your clamps may leave marks on the surface of your project.

An inexpensive addition to your workshop, "C" clamps are useful for many woodworking applications. One end of their C-shaped frame is fixed; the other end is fitted with a threaded rod and swivel pad that can be clamped tightly across an opening ranging from zero to several inches or more, depending upon the size of the clamp. C-clamps can hold two thicknesses of wood together, secure a piece of wood to a work surface, and perform many other functions.

Bar clamps and pipe clamps are used to hold assemblies together temporarily while you add the fasteners, as well as to apply pressure when boards are glued together edge-to-edge. While pipe clamps look very much the same and serve the same purposes, they're significantly less expensive. The fittings, which you buy separately from the pipes, can be slipped onto pipes of various lengths, depending upon your needs. Rubber "shoes" for pipe-clamp fittings will protect your projects and are widely available.

Web clamps (or band clamps) are used for clamping such things as chairs or drawers; they exert a uniform pressure completely around a project. The "clamp" actually consists of a continuous band of flexible material such as nylon strapping, with an attached metal ratchet mechanism that pulls the band tightly around the object to be clamped.

MEASURING TOOLS

"Measure twice—cut once," is the oldest expression in woodworking, and it's sound advice. Accurate cutting depends on accurate measuring, so by paying particular attention to accurate measuring, you'll ensure that your project will fit together perfectly during final assembly. To make your job easier, purchase high-quality measuring tools. A wide, steel tape measure is a good choice for most projects. (A narrow tape will bend more easily along the length of a board and will be less accurate.)

A level does what its name suggests—help you determine whether a surface is level. In its steel casing is a small liquid-filled tube with an air-bubble trapped in the liquid. When the bubble centers over a line on the casing, the surface on which the level is sitting is indeed level.

When you're checking your work surface for level, set a fairly long level in various places on it, turning the level each time so you're gauging the level in several different directions. If you notice variations, shim the legs or the areas just underneath the work surface with a piece of wood thick enough to make the surface level. Attach the shim with glue and with nails or screws to make certain that it stays in place while you work.

A straightedge (a steel ruler, 12" or 24" long) is a handy tool for taking quick measurements and for marking straight lines.

A sliding T-bevel, used to check, transfer and mark bevels and miters, consists of a steel blade that pivots and slides within a handle. The blade can be locked in position to form an angle.

Squares are versatile and essential tools in woodworking. The most commonly used types are the framing (or carpenter's) square and the combination square. In addition to their obvious uses (marking a cutting line on a board and obtaining a right angle), squares can be used to check the outer or inner squareness of a joint, to guide a saw through a cut, and much more. The illustrations on the next page show how to use a combination square to mark crosscuts and rip cuts.

Use the same measuring device consistently throughout any given project; two different instruments may vary enough to give you slightly different measurements.

MARKING A CROSSCUT

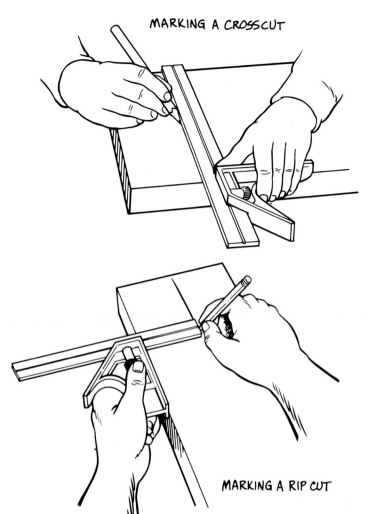

MARKING A RIP CUT

CUTTING TOOLS

The thickness of a saw blade is called its *kerf*. Why is this important? Because every time you use a blade to cut wood, it removes an amount of wood equal to its kerf. (Whence cometh the gigantic amount of sawdust that accumulates when you make a project.) When you measure and mark your boards, mark your cut to the waste side (the side you don't care about) of the board. Then, when you're ready to make the cut, position the saw blade so that it precisely removes the mark, and your cut will always be accurate.

A piece of wood may be *ripped* (cut along its length) or crosscut (cut across its width). Specific saws or saw blades exist for each procedure. A rip saw has teeth designed for cutting along the length of board, with the grain. This saw comes with 4-1/2 through 7 points per inch, the latter giving the smoothest cut. A crosscut saw is made to cut across the grain and is available with 7 through 12 points per inch, depending on how coarse or fine you wish the cut to be. The greater the number, the smoother the cut.

Probably the most popular power-cutting tool is the circular saw, the blade of which can be adjusted to cut at a 90-degree or 45-degree angle, or at any angle in between. While power-tool saw blades for ripping and crosscutting are also available, the most practical circular-saw blade for general woodworking is a combination blade, which will rip or crosscut with equal ease. Carbide-tipped blades are more expensive, but they're well worth the cost because they last much longer than regular blades.

The hand-held jig or sabre saw is a power saw used to cut curves, shapes, and large holes in panels or boards up to 1-1/2" in thickness. Its cutting action comes from a narrow reciprocating "bayonet" blade that moves up and down very quickly. The best sabre saws have a variable speed control and an orbital blade action; the blade swings forward into the work and back again during its up-and-down cycle. An attached dust blower keeps the sawdust away from the cut.

Whenever you cut either lumber or plywood, note the type of cut that your tool is making and use it to your advantage. For example, circular saws and saber saws cut on the upstroke, so they may leave ragged edges on the upper surface of your wood. When cutting with these saws, position the wood with the better surface facing down.

Certain types of cuts, such as hollowing out a section of wood, are made with chisels. Although learning to use chisels well takes some practice, it's worth the effort because these tools can perform unique woodworking tasks. Always work with sharp chisels. For your first purchase, choose two different sizes: one very narrow and one about 1" wide.

For shaving just a little wood from the end or the edge of a board, a plane is the appropriate tool to use. Again, buy a high-quality plane, and practice with it until you become fairly proficient.

DRILL AND BITS

A hand or power drill with an assortment of bits is a necessity for almost any woodworking task. A 3/8" variable-speed reversible drill is one of the most valuable power tools you'll ever own and isn't very expensive, either. For more information on using a drill and on the bits that will come in handiest, turn to pages 21-22.

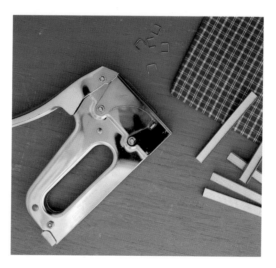

STAPLES AND STAPLE GUNS

Staples are light-duty fasteners and are often used to attach fabric to wood. A staple gun is a worthwhile investment and a handy piece of equipment to have around the house. The guns are available in many sizes and prices. Although electric models are convenient, a heavy-duty, hand-operated staple gun will probably be all that you need. Purchase staples in a variety of lengths so that you'll have the size you need to accommodate different materials.

remove by hand sanding. A finishing sander is probably the most practical power sander for furniture projects. This tool will smooth surfaces quickly and will not leave circular marks.

A hand-held, power belt sander is often used for large jobs, as it sands very quickly, but because it's so powerful, this tool is difficult to control on softwood such as pine. A belt sander can easily gouge softwood, and unless you watch it carefully, can remove more wood than you wish.

No matter what sanding tool you use, begin with coarse sandpaper to remove the worst of the roughness and then gradually progress to sandpaper with a fine grit.

SANDERS

Any project may be sanded by hand. An inexpensive plastic sanding block will do the job of sanding a level surface just fine; it holds the sandpaper taut and flat and saves wear on your bare hand. You can even substitute a block of wood by wrapping a piece of sandpaper around it. To sand moldings and curves, try wrapping a pencil or another appropriately sized object with sandpaper.

The amount of sanding required for each project depends both on how you'll be using the project and on what kind of finish you plan to apply. Obviously, a rustic project won't need to be sanded completely smooth. A rustic chair, however, will require more sanding than a rustic cabinet—someone will be sitting on the chair! An indoor cabinet that you've decided to stain should be sanded more than one you want to paint.

An orbital sander does a good job of beginning the sanding process, but it may leave circular marks that you'll need to

MATERIALS AND SUPPLIES

LUMBER

A piece of wood is a piece of wood—right? Not exactly. Each wood possesses its own unique characteristics; each tree, for example, has different grain patterns and fiber density. Some woods are very light (balsa, for example), and some woods, such as ebony, are extremely heavy. The odor of cedar repels moths, and redwood is insect-resistant. Knowing some facts about wood will enable you to choose the right wood for your project.

All woods are classified as either hardwood or softwood. Hardwood comes from deciduous trees such as maple, cherry, and walnut, which shed their leave every year. Softwood is cut from coniferous trees (or evergreens) such as pine, redwood, and cedar.

As its name implies, softwood is generally easier to cut, drill, and nail than is hardwood. It's also much less expensive, so it's a good choice for the beginning woodworker.

Softwood is sold in standard dimensional sizes such as 2 x 4 and 1 x 12, and in specific lengths such as 6', 8', and 10'. The bin labeled 2 x 4 x 8 at your local building-supply store contains 2 x 4 boards that are 8' long.

While it might appear that a 2 x 4 should be 2" thick and 4" wide, this is not the case. The rough board was 2" x 4" before it was planed to a smooth surface on all four sides. After surfacing, a 2 x 4 actually measures 1-1/2" x 3-1/2". The chart below shows the *nominal* sizes (what the board is called) and the *actual* measurements of dimensional lumber.

Nominal Size	Actual Dimensions
1 x 2	3/4" x 1-1/2"
1 x 3	3/4" x 2-1/2"
1 x 4	3/4" x 3-1/2"
1 x 6	3/4" x 5-1/2"
1 x 8	3/4" x 7-1/4"
1 x 10	3/4" x 9-1/4"
1 x 12	3/4" x 11-1/4"
2 x 2	1-1/2" x 1-1/2"
2 x 4	1-1/2" x 3-1/2"
2 x 6	1-1/2" x 5-1/2"
2 x 8	1/1-2" x 7-1/4"
2 x 10	1-1/2" x 9-1/4"
2 x 12	1-1/2" x 11-1/4"
4 x 4	3-1/2" x 3-1/2"
4 x 6	3-1/2" x 3-1/2"
6 x 6	5-1/2" x 5-1/2"
8 x 8	7-1/4" x 7-1/4"

Because lumberyards and building-supply stores purchase lumber from different sources, individual boards of the same nominal size may not always be the same actual width—even if you purchase them at the same store at the same time. A slight difference in the width or thickness of the boards will mean that your project won't fit together correctly, so take time in the store to check the wood that you buy. A few extra pre-purchase minutes will save many headaches later.

The price of softwood is directly related to its quality. "Select" wood is a better grade than "common" and therefore costs more. Don't buy a higher-quality wood than you really need. While you wouldn't want knots in the lumber for a coffee table, a few knots probably won't bother you if you're building an outdoor planter. Following are descriptions of softwood grades:

COMMON GRADES

No. 1 common: contains knots and a few imperfections, but should have no knotholes

No. 2 common: free of knotholes, but contains some knots

No. 3 common: contains larger knots and small knotholes

No. 4 common: used for construction only; contains large knotholes

No. 5 common: lowest grade of lumber; used only when strength and good appearance aren't necessary

SELECT GRADES

B and better (or 1 and 2 clear): the best and most expensive grades; used for the finest furniture projects

C select: may have a few small blemishes

D select: the lowest quality of the better board grades; imperfections can be concealed with paint

The "clear" boards (see "Select Grades") come from the inner section of the tree (the heartwood) and are nearly free of imperfections. The sapwood (or outer portions of the tree) yields boards with more knots and other flaws.

Examine each piece of wood that you purchase for imperfections. If you intend to paint your finished project, small, tight knots are acceptable. Avoid wood with large knotholes, as they'll often fall out of the wood later, leaving a giant hole behind. You can sometimes eliminate knots on the ends of otherwise good boards by simply cutting them off, but remember to purchase extra to allow for the waste.

The biggest problem with wood is that it has a tendency to warp and bow. Straightening a warped piece of wood is possible, but is a prolonged procedure; purchasing wood that is already straight is much easier. The best way to check for warping or bowing is to place one end of the board on the floor and look down the length of its face. Then turn the board and look down its edge. Any warps or bows will be immediately obvious.

Also avoid boards that are split—either at an end or elsewhere. Splits tend to enlarge, eventually resulting in two pieces of wood rather than one, and neither piece will be useable. If the split is at an end and is very short, simply cut off the split portion, but again, be sure to allow for the waste.

Although selecting boards is tedious, it will prevent much frustration later. Some lumberyards won't allow you to "hand pick" wood in this manner—shop somewhere else.

Before you cut individual pieces of lumber, re-inspect each board. If you have an 8'-long board, for example, and you need a 7-1/2'-long piece, check for knots at either end and eliminate the 6" length that contains the knots. Also plan your cuts so that the better face of the wood will end up on the outside of your finished project. Doing this will save you time during the filling and sanding procedures and will reward you with a more attractive project.

All of the projects in this book can be built with hardwood, but because hardwoods are usually sold in random widths and lengths, you'll need to make some extra calculations. Each hardwood board is cut from the log as wide and as long as possible. Consequently, hardwood is sold by a measure called the *board foot*. A board foot represents a piece of lumber 1" (or less) thick, 12" wide, and 12" long. Hardwood thicknesses are measured in quarter inches. The standard thicknesses are 3/4, 4/4, 5/4, 6/4, and 8/4. The board-foot measurement is doubled for boards thicker than 1".

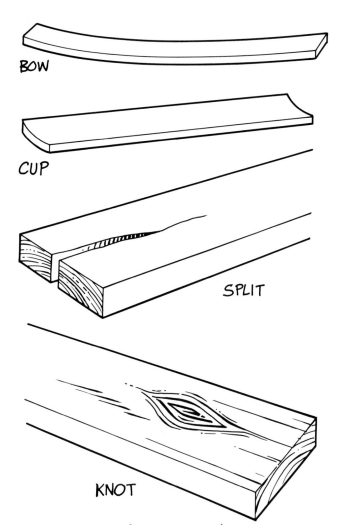

BOW

CUP

SPLIT

KNOT

Plywood, as you might guess, is made from several plies of wood that are glued together and is generally sold in sheets measuring 4' x 8', although some stores also stock half-sheets measuring 4' x 4'. Plywood comes in standard thicknesses of 1/8", 1/4", 3/8", 1/2", 5/8", and 3/4".

There are two principal kinds of plywood: veneer-core and lumber-core. Lumber-core is the higher quality material; its edges can be worked as you would work solid wood. Because the exposed cut edges of veneer-core plywood are unsightly, they must be filled with wood filler or covered with wood trim.

Plywood is also graded according to the quality of the outer veneer. The grades are "A" through "D," with "A" representing the best quality. Each piece of plywood has two designations—one for each face. An "A-D" piece, for example, has one veneered surface that is "A" quality and one that is "D" quality.

If plywood is designated as "exterior-grade," the glue between its plies is waterproof. Don't use interior-grade plywood to construct outdoor projects or for indoor projects that will be exposed to a lot of moisture.

WOOD JOINTS

Different kinds of wood joints count in the hundreds. They range in complexity from the plainest butt joint to incredibly intricate and time-consuming joints used only by master woodworkers. The projects in this book are constructed with the simplest joints and are secured with glue and nails or screws.

Edge-to-edge joint: You'll use this joint when you're laminating boards together edge-to-edge to make a wider piece of wood. To ensure a perfect joint between boards, first rip a minuscule amount from each edge of each board. Next, apply glue to the adjoining edges and clamp the boards together firmly, applying even pressure along their lengths. Don't overtighten the clamps; if you do, the glue will be forced out or the lamination may start to bow across its width. To prevent bowing on a long lamination, place extra boards above and below the lamination, across its width, and clamp those boards with C-clamps or wood clamps. Wipe off any excess glue that is squeezed out during the clamping process.

Butt joint: This simple joint, in which one board abuts another at a right angle, offers the least holding power of any. Butt joints must be reinforced with fasteners of some kind—usually screws.

Miter: A miter is an angle cut across the width of a board and is used to join two pieces of wood so that the end grain of neither piece is exposed. A mitered joint must also be reinforced with nails or screws. The angle most often cut is 45 degrees. When two 45-degree-mitered boards are joined together, they form a 90-degree angle.

Bevel: A bevel is an angular cut along the length of a board, rather than across the width as in a miter.

Dado: A dado is a groove cut in the face of one board to accommodate the thickness of another board. Dadoes may be cut with a saw and chisel, with a router, or with a dado set on a table saw.

No matter what kind of joint you're making, use both glue and fasteners (nails or screws) whenever possible. The only exception is on joints that you wish to disassemble at a later time; omit the glue on these.

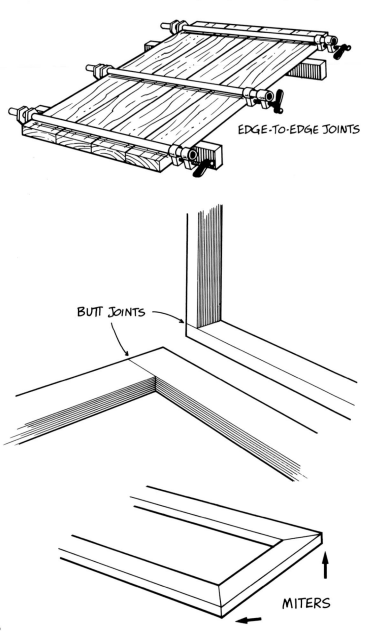

EDGE-TO-EDGE JOINTS

BUTT JOINTS

MITERS

You may wish to pre-assemble your project without using glue, especially if you're a beginner. This process—known as *dry-fitting*—will allow you to make certain that all of the pieces were cut correctly and will fit together tightly. Use clamps to hold the pieces together temporarily or hammer small nails into the surface just far enough to hold them in place. (Leave a large portion of each nail head above the surface, so that removing the nails will be easy.) After checking the fit, adjust the pieces as necessary. Then remove the clamps and/or nails, apply glue, and reassemble the pieces.

ADHESIVES

For interior projects, ordinary, straw-colored carpenter's glue (aliphatic resin) is the optimum choice. For exterior use, a nontoxic waterproof wood glue is a better choice. The pre-catalyzed aliphatic resin now on the market offers the same advantages as the yellow carpenter's glue, but it resists the effects of water and weather. If this type of adhesive isn't available, you may use the more costly two-part resorcinol, but the latter takes about 12 hours to set and at least another 12 hours to cure completely. For some projects, such as those in which tile is attached to wood, paneling-and-construction adhesive works well.

Don't overdo the amount of glue you apply, as the excess glue will be squeezed out when the joint is clamped or fastened and will drip all over your project. I usually apply a small ribbon of glue down the center of one surface and then rub the adjoining surface against the ribbon to distribute the glue evenly. Your objective is to coat both surfaces with a uniform, thin coating. If you do encounter drips, wipe them off quickly with a damp cloth; dry glue is difficult to remove. Because glue also rejects most stains, you'll have to sand off any on exposed surfaces of the project.

NAILS

Although there are many different types of nails (common, large flathead, duplex head, and oval head among others), the one most commonly used in woodworking is the finishing nail. This nail has a much smaller

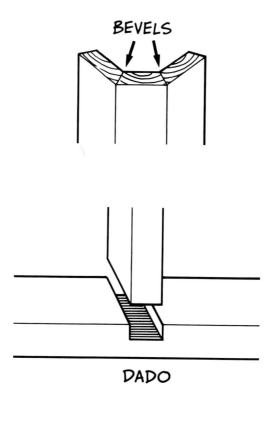

BEVELS

DADO

CUT DADO TO DEPTH WITH SAW

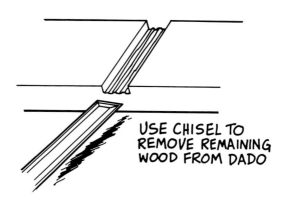

USE CHISEL TO REMOVE REMAINING WOOD FROM DADO

head than the common nail and is therefore easy to recess below the surface of the wood—a process known as *countersinking*. Countersunk nails are easily concealed by filling the holes above them with wood filler.

Nail sizes, designated by "penny" (abbreviated as "d"), correspond directly to nail lengths. The diameter of the nail gets larger as the nail gets longer. Finishing nails range in length from 1" to 6". Some of the more commonly-used sizes are listed in the table that follows:

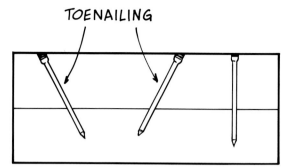

TOENAILING

Penny Size	Nail Length
2d	1"
3d	1-1/4"
4d	1-1/2"
5d	1-3/4"
6d	2"
7d	2-1/4"
8d	2-1/2"
9d	2-3/4"
10d	3"
12d	3-1/4"
16d	3-1/2"
20d	4"

As a general rule, when you're joining two pieces of wood together, use a nail that's as long as possible but not one so long that it will penetrate the opposite surface; the longer the nail, the greater the holding power. When joining two 1 x 4s (each of which is 3/4" thick), for example, use a 1-1/4" nail. The nail will penetrate all but 1/4" of the 1-1/2" thickness of the combined boards.

When possible, drive nails in at an angle rather than straight into the work; angled nails provide more holding power. Driving a nail into the wood at an extreme angle to secure two pieces together is referred to as *toenailing*.

The most difficult part of toenailing comes when you've hammered the nail almost entirely into the wood and only the head and a bit of the shank are visible. In order to avoid making hammer marks in the

wood as you drive the remaining nail section in, use a nail set to finish the job and to countersink the nail. In fact, it's wise to use a nail set on all finishing nails. The trick to using this tool effectively is to hold it firmly with all four fingers and your thumb. Rest your little finger on the surface of the wood for added stability.

Hardwood and very narrow pieces of softwood have a tendency to split when you drive nails into them. To avoid this problem, pre-drill the nail holes first, using a drill bit slightly smaller than the diameter of the nail. Drill the pilot hole about two-thirds the length of the nail, and then drive the nail into it.

Use only galvanized nails on projects that will be placed out-of-doors. When ordinary nails are exposed to the elements, they'll stain the wood a black color, ruining the appearance of your project.

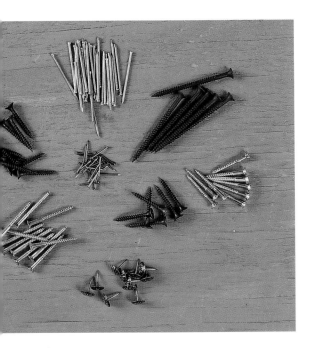

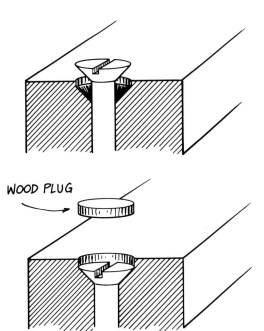

WOOD PLUG

SCREWS

Screws have more holding power than nails, and when they're used without glue, the pieces they fasten can be separated easily at a later date. The disadvantage of screws is that they aren't as easy to insert.

The type of screw most often used in woodworking is called a flathead screw. The flat surface of its head can be countersunk below the surface of the wood. The modern drywall (or sharp-point woodworking screw) is an improvement on the old standard because it's designed to be used with a power driver.

Screws are designated by their diameter (provided as a gauge number) and their length—#6 x 1-1/4", for example. Common sizes range from #2 to #16, with larger diameters having higher gauge numbers. Use screws as large in diameter as is possible without splitting the wood and as long as possible without penetrating the opposite surface.

Pre-drilling holes for countersunk screws is normally a two-step operation. First, a pilot hole is drilled, using a drill bit the same diameter as the threaded portion of the screw minus its threads. Then a larger, countersunk hole, slightly larger in diameter than the screw head, is centered and drilled over the pilot hole to accommodate the head of the screw. If you use the same size screws on a regular basis, you may wish to invest in a combination pilot-countersink bit for your drill, which will perform both countersinking operations at the same time.

The countersunk portion of the hole can be just deep enough to allow the head of the screw to sink slightly below the wood surface, or it can be deep enough to accommodate both the screw head and a wood plug inserted on top of the screw head. Wood plugs can be purchased or made by cutting off slices from a wooden dowel rod. The only disadvantage to the sliced dowel plugs is that the exposed end grain of each slice will be noticeable if you stain the wood. An alternative is to cut your own plugs using a plug cutter—a bit that fits into and is powered by an electric drill.

When you're working on very soft wood, it's possible to countersink a screw simply by driving it in with a power drill, but you'll

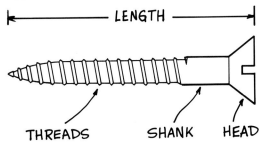

 LENGTH

THREADS   SHANK   HEAD

need to fill the resulting surface hole with wood filler or with a wood plug.

Screws can be inserted at an angle, the same way that nails are, to "toenail" two pieces of wood together. After some practice, you'll be able to start a screw at any angle with very little or no effort. To make this easier, use a drill or a screw starter to start a hole for the screw.

Although you don't want to add so many screws to your project that the metal outweighs the wood, don't be stingy with them. If there's the slightest chance that a joint could be shaky, I add a couple of extra screws. The project you're making will probably be subjected to several moves over the course of its lifetime—either to different rooms or to different houses—and these moves will place additional strain on the joints.

BRADS AND TACKS

Wire brads—smaller and thinner versions of finishing nails—are used to attach trim or very small project pieces. Their lengths are designated in inches and their diameters in wire-gauge numbers ranging from 11 to 20. The lower the gauge number, the larger the diameter of the brad.

Tacks have large heads and are used to attach fabric or other materials to wood when light fastening is all that is required. The large-diameter head can be strictly ornamental, or it can be used to hold something lightly in place.

PAINTS, STAINS, AND VARNISHES

When you select a finish, keep in mind where the project will live. Although latex-based finishes are easy to clean up with water, projects that will occupy kitchens or other humid environments should be finished with a protective coat of polyurethane or spar varnish.

As a matter of personal preference, I always use non-toxic finishes. You should always use these when you build projects for children's rooms. Finish all outdoor projects with an exterior-grade stain or paint, and seal them with a weather-proof sealer.

Before using any product, read the directions carefully and follow them explicitly.

Before you paint any project, apply a coat of sealer in order to seal the wood surfaces and prevent knotholes or other imperfections from weeping through the paint. In the long run, using a sealer will save time and materials, as sealers eliminate the need for multiple coats of paint.

Although some professionals will only use very expensive hog-bristle brushes, I never buy any brush that must be cleaned. I've become addicted to inexpensive sponge brushes, which can be thrown in the trash when you're through with a job. Don't buy the ones that look like kitchen sponges, with visible holes on their surfaces. Look, instead, for the ones resembling cosmetic sponges; their surfaces will appear smooth.

One last hint on finishing: when you need to stop your painting or staining in the middle of the job, just pop your brush into an airtight sandwich bag. It won't dry out even if you leave it there overnight.

SAFETY

Bear in mind that working with power tools can be dangerous. I know many wood-workers, and some of them have missing digits. If that news frightens you, so much the better; it only takes one careless action to result in frightful consequences.

This book is written for beginning wood-workers who possess a minimum number of hand tools. If you'd like to use stationary power tools as well, make certain that you know what you're doing. Read the instructions that come with your tools very carefully, and never attempt any woodworking maneuver that can't be performed safely with the tools you have. Misuse of power tools can lead to damaged tools and serious injury to yourself.

Never take your eyes off the work at hand. Concentrate on what you're doing, and take the necessary safety precautions. Develop the habit of avoiding the path of a saw; don't stand directly behind it or directly in front of it. Power saws can flip a piece of wood at you with incredible force.

Wear safety goggles when you're working with wood. One splinter of wood flying toward your eye will make the purchase price and the practice of donning goggles worth your while.

The amount of sawdust produced when you work with wood makes some sort of dust mask a prudent accessory. Wood dust can be very irritating to your lungs. A number of different masks are available, ranging from simple paper masks to more sophisticated masks with replaceable filters.

Prolonged exposure to loud noise can have harmful effects on your hearing. If you use power tools for extended periods—especially power saws, which can be quite loud—a pair of ear plugs or protectors is a good investment.

Practicing all of these safety rules will ensure that your woodworking activities are pleasurable.

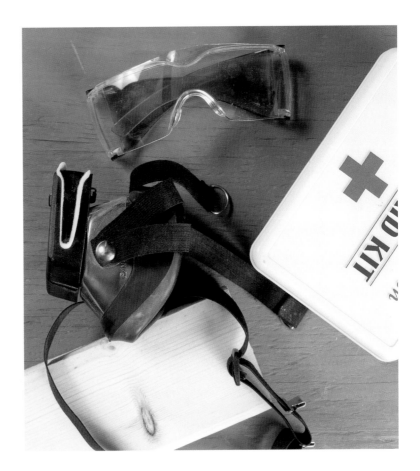

THE PROJECTS

You're probably ready to dash out and buy materials for your first project, but before you do, quell your enthusiasm just long enough to read this section. In it, you'll find essential information on how the project instructions and lists are organized—information that will save you both time and money.

Every project in this book comes with helpful lists and many also include special tips. Here's how the information within each project is arranged:

SKILL LEVEL

If you'd like to know how difficult a project is likely to be before you tackle it, look for the "Skill Level" code included with each one. If you see one hammer, you'll know the project is easy to construct. Two hammers identifies a project as a bit more challenging, and three hammers puts a project in the challenging category. Don't think that challenging means impossible-for-beginners, though; it doesn't. Think of three hammers as three reminders: Take your time, take care to measure and cut accurately, and take breaks if you get impatient or tired.

SPECIAL TOOLS AND TECHNIQUES

I've added this list to the projects that require tools you may not own—and/or skills you may not have. If you see "mitering" in this list, and you've never cut a miter in your life, look up "miters" in the index on page 128, read the appropriate section, and take the time to practice cutting a few miters on scrap wood before you begin the project.

Advanced woodworkers who'd like to build these projects using stationary power tools should be very careful when modifying instructions to accommodate these tools. The procedures used when working with hand tools may not be the same (or safe) when you switch to heavy-duty power tools, so know the capabilities of your tools and don't exceed them.

MATERIALS AND SUPPLIES

As well as naming necessary supplies, this list specifies the amount of wood you'll need in total linear feet. Let's say the list specifies 23 linear feet of 1 x 4 pine. You have at least two options: You can buy two 1 x 4s, each 12' long; or you can purchase four 1 x 4s, each 6' long. Read through the "Cutting List" and instructions before you make these decisions.

For purposes of clarity in the project instructions, each board surface has been named. The broadest part of the board is called its face, and the narrow surface along the length of the board is its edge. The ends, obviously, are the smallest surfaces at each end of the board.

HARDWARE

Here you'll find listed every piece of hardware that you need for the project you've chosen.

CUTTING LIST

This list will let you know the exact size of each piece you'll need to cut from the wood you buy. Don't cut the pieces right away; the instructions will walk you through cutting each piece step-by-step. Do, however, read through this list and the project instructions before you shop for materials. You certainly don't want to buy all of your 1 x 4s in 6' lengths if your project calls for a piece 7-1/2' long.

When you get to the store, inspect the various lengths of wood available. The 6'-long boards may be knotted or warped, while the 12' lengths are nearly perfect; in this case, it makes sense to buy the longer boards. Wise choices will be easier to make if you've read the instructions before you get to the store.

Buy a bit more wood than you think you'll need—perhaps 10 to 20 percent more. Having to return to the store for another 2 x 4 because you miscut the last one you had is a frustrating experience. Keep in mind that the ends of boards aren't always square, so you'll need to allow for having to square off the ends before you begin measuring. You can always use the wood that's left over when you build the next project.

Also bear in mind that you'll have to transport the lumber back home. You may be able to fit 4'-long boards into the trunk of your car, but do you have a way to haul 12'-long boards? If not, ask the store to cut them for you; most suppliers won't charge for the first cut.

Consider the type of finish that you want to apply to the completed project, too. Projects that you plan to paint can be built with lower grades of wood, as wood filler and paint will cover many imperfections in the lumber. For projects that you plan to stain, however, pay particular attention to the grain of the wood that you're buying; choose better-quality boards with similar grain patterns.

When you begin the actual cutting, start with the longest boards. If you miscut, you'll still have plenty of wood left to cut another piece, and you can recut the miscut board to make the shorter pieces.

ONE FINAL TIP

Every fine woodworker has blackened a thumb with a hammer, cut a board too short, or drilled a hole with the wrong bit. Think of these sorts of slip-ups—and you'll make your share—not as cues to quit your new hobby, but as clues. Your throbbing thumb, for example, may be telling you that your projects will look better if you build them when you're rested and alert! Take a break, relax, and start over.

HOUSE NUMBERS

Here's a quick and easy way to add a face-lift to the outside of your house: Replace those old house numbers from the hardware store with this great-looking project. The numbered tiles are readily available at most building-supply stores. To give our project some pizazz, we added a border of 1"-square tiles to the design.

SPECIAL TOOLS AND TECHNIQUES

Small mastic trowel

Rubber-surfaced grout trowel

Mitering

MATERIALS AND SUPPLIES

9 linear feet of 1 x 4 pine

1 piece of 3/4"-thick plywood, 22" x 26"

9 linear feet of 3/4"-wide decorative molding

2 pieces of 3/4" x 3/4" scrap wood, 22" long

2 pieces of 3/4" x 3/4" scrap wood, 26" long

House-number tiles

1" x 1" border tiles (optional)

Small containers of tile grout, mastic, and sealer

HARDWARE

Approximately 20 #6 x 1-1/4" flathead wood screws

Approximately 30 wire brads

CUTTING LIST

Code	Description	Qty.	Material	Dimensions
A	Base	1	3/4" plywood	Cut to fit
B	Side	2	1 x 4 pine	Cut to fit
C	Top/Bottom	2	1 x 4 pine	Cut to fit

NOTES ON MATERIALS

Purchase exterior-grade plywood for the base (A), and if you plan to place your finished project outdoors, be sure to use exterior-grade wood components and galvanized hardware. Also be sure to use paint, grout, and sealer that are rated for exterior use.

Because the number of digits in house numbers varies, so will the total number of tiles and the amount of wood you need; this project must be personalized for each residence. The materials specified here will be sufficient for a tile design that measures 20" x 24", or less. If your design is larger, just add to the wood materials specified. If you decide to include the border tiles, buy a few extra in case you break any of them.

Most tiles sold at building-supply stores are now "self-spacing"; they come with small projections on their edges so that when you lay them out, the grout lines between the tiles will be even. We suggest that you spend some time at the tile supplier laying out the numbered tiles—and the border tiles if you decide to use them—to make certain that you like the design and that it completes a rectangle. The exact size doesn't matter; all of the wood pieces can be adjusted to fit.

CUTTING THE PLYWOOD

1. In order to determine the precise size of your project, you'll need to lay out your design on the 3/4"-thick plywood. Place the tiles on the plywood exactly as you want them to look in the finished project, making certain that they're spaced correctly and that the sides of the tile rectangle are absolutely straight. If your tiles aren't self-spacing, don't forget to leave gaps for the grout.

2. Place a 3/4" x 3/4" piece of scrap wood along each of the four sides of the tile design. The scrap wood will align the tiles and will add a 3/4" width on all four sides. Use a framing square to make certain that the outer edges of the four scrap pieces are exactly square with one another.

3. Use a pencil to mark the outer perimeter of the scrap wood onto the plywood. To form the plywood base (A) of the project, carefully cut out the marked rectangle.

4. Cut four pieces of 3/4"-wide decorative molding to fit exactly around the perimeter of the upper face of the base (A), mitering the corners of the molding as shown in *Figure 1*. Check to see that the tiled design

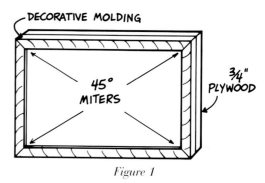

Figure 1

will fit exactly inside the decorative molding that you have cut—now is the time to make any necessary adjustments.

5. Glue the mitered decorative molding to the upper face of the base (A) and secure it with small wire brads. Use a tack hammer to insert the brads and recess them into the molding with a nail set.

6. Measure the length and width of the base (A). Cut two sides (B) from 1 x 4 pine to the exact width of the rectangle.

7. Add 1-1/2" to the length of the rectangle and cut two top/bottom pieces (C) from 1 x 4 pine to that measurement.

8. Place the two sides (B) on one top/bottom piece (C), as shown in *Figure 2*. Make certain that the assembly is perfectly square. Glue the pieces together and insert two 1-1/4" screws through the top/bottom piece (C) and into the side (B) at each joint.

9. Fit the plywood assembly into the two sides (B) and top/bottom piece (C), as shown in *Figure 3*, adjusting the plywood so that it is inset 1-1/2" from the back edges of the sides and top/bottom piece.

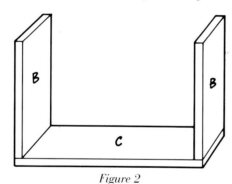

Figure 2

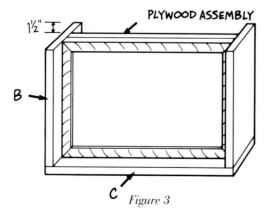

Figure 3

10. Glue the remaining top/bottom piece (C) to the two sides (B) and secure it in place with two 1-1/4" screws at each joint.

11. To hold the plywood assembly in place, insert three 1-1/4" screws through each side (B) and each top/bottom piece (C) into the edges of the plywood.

FINISHING THE WOOD FRAME

1. Fill any holes, cracks, or crevices with wood filler.

2. Sand the project thoroughly.

3. Paint the wood frame the color of your choice. Do not paint the plywood face that will receive the tiles.

ADDING THE TILES

1. Following the manufacturer's directions carefully, use a small trowel to spread an even coat of tile mastic over the surface of the plywood base. Take care not to get the mastic on any of the painted decorative molding.

2. Place the tiles on the mastic one at a time, making sure that they are absolutely straight. Do not slide them, or the mastic will be forced up onto the sides of the tiles. Let the mastic dry overnight.

3. Mix the tile grout according to the manufacturer's directions (or use pre-mixed grout).

4. Using a rubber-surfaced grout trowel, spread the grout over the tiles with arc-like motions. Hold the trowel at an angle so that it forces the grout evenly into the spaces between the tiles.

5. When the grout begins to set up, use a damp rag to wipe the excess from the tiles and the joints. Don't let the grout dry completely before doing this, or it will be very difficult to remove. Use as little water as possible during this process so that you don't thin the grout that remains. Let the grout dry overnight.

6. Wipe the remaining film from the tiles with a damp rag.

7. Apply grout sealer, following the manufacturer's directions. (These directions often recommend that you wait several days before applying the sealer to the project.)

Victorian Table

The four decorative quarter-circles that make up the surface of this lovely table were originally destined for use as gingerbread on house porches, but you'll use them—and a circular sheet of glass—to transform an easy-to-make stand into a lovely table. Once you've purchased the materials, you can probably construct the entire project in a couple of hours. Paint the finished table, add the glass to the top, and you're finished.

Materials and Supplies

1 sheet of 3/4"-thick plywood, 4' x 8'
4 decorative gingerbread quarter-circles
1 circle of 3/8"-thick glass, 36" in diameter
5 small felt or plastic pads to protect the glass

Hardware

Approximately 30 #6 x 1-1/4" flathead wood screws

Cutting List

Code	Description	Qty.	Material	Dimensions
A	Table support	2	3/4" plywood	29" x 35-1/4"

Notes on Materials

For a table the same size as the one shown in the photo, the straight sides of each gingerbread quarter-circle that you purchase should measure 17-1/4". If you'd like to use larger or smaller quarter-circles, just alter the measurements of the plywood to match the size of the gingerbread that you find.

When you buy the circular piece of glass, be sure that its edges have been beveled or sanded in some manner so that no one is injured by sharp glass.

The table supports (A) will support a glass circle of up to 40" in diameter.

Constructing the Table

1. The two-piece stand fits together by means of a slot system (see *Figure 1*). First cut two 29" x 35-1/4" table supports (A) from 3/4"-thick plywood. Then carefully cut the slot in the center of each table support (A). Be certain that you make these cuts very carefully, or the table supports will not fit together correctly.

2. Apply glue to the inner edges of the cut slots. Then fit the slots in the two table supports (A) together so that the supports form an X shape when viewed from above.

Figure 2

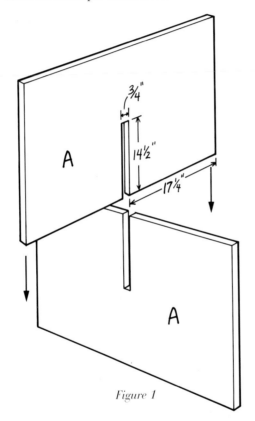

Figure 1

3. The quarter-circles are fastened in the openings between the table supports (A), with their upper surfaces flush with the upper edges of the supports, as shown in *Figure 2*. Apply glue to both straight edges of one quarter-circle and position it between two adjacent table supports (A). Fasten the quarter-circle in place by inserting three 1-1/4" screws through the table support (A) and into the gingerbread; place one screw as close as possible to each end of the support and one in the

middle. Repeat to fasten the other edge of the quarter-circle to the other support.

4. Repeat Step 3 to attach another quarter-circle opposite to the one you attached in the last step. Then attach the remaining two quarter-circles. You'll need to angle the screws into these last two quarter-circles from underneath the previously attached quarter-circles next to them.

Finishing

1. Fill any holes, cracks, or crevices with wood filler.

2. Paint or stain the table the color of your choice.

3. Affix the five small felt or plastic pads to the upper edges of the table support, as shown in the photo of the table without glass. These will protect the lower surface of the glass and will prevent the glass from sliding out of place.

4. Place the circular glass on top of the table.

TILED LAMP

This project was made as a present for my neighbor Patti, who needed a lamp for her kitchen desk but who couldn't find an attractive one that was short enough to fit under her cabinets. Because Patti had several kitchen tiles left over from a decorating project, we decided to use them on the lamp.

SPECIAL TECHNIQUES

Beveling

MATERIALS AND SUPPLIES

4 linear feet of 1 x 6 pine

2 linear feet of 1 x 8 pine

1 small tube of paneling-and-construction adhesive

8 ceramic tiles, each 4" x 4"

1 lamp shade

4 small felt or plastic pads for the bottom of the lamp base

HARDWARE

Approximately 10 3d finishing nails

Approximately 40 wire brads

Lamp kit (See "Notes on Materials")

Cutting List

Code	Description	Qty.	Material	Dimensions
A	Side	4	1 x 6 pine	9-1/2" long
B	Top/Bottom	2	1 x 8 pine	7-1/4" long

Notes on Materials

Lamp kits, consisting of all the hardware necessary to wire a lamp, are carried by most building-supply stores. Purchase the shade, which is not included with the kit, after your project is finished. When you shop for the shade, take the completed project with you and try several different shades while you're at the store.

Constructing the Base

1. The lamp base has four identical 9-1/2"-long sides (A), which are cut from a single length of beveled 1 x 6 pine. To make the sides, first cut a 40" length of 1 x 6 and bevel both its long edges at a 45-degree angle, as shown in *Figure 1*.

2. Cut four 9-1/2"-long sides (A) from the beveled 1 x 6.

3. Glue together the beveled edges of the four sides (A) to form a hollow rectangle measuring 5-1/2" x 9-1/2", as shown in *Figure 2*. Secure the four sides by driving four wire brads through the beveled edges along each side of each joint.

4. Cut two top/bottom pieces (B) from 1 x 8 pine, each 7-1/4" long.

5. Center one top/bottom piece (B) over one open end of the hollow rectangular base and glue it in place. Insert one 3d finishing nail through the top/bottom and into the end of each side (A).

6. Repeat Step 5 to attach the other top/bottom piece (B) to the other end of the hollow rectangular base.

7. Fill any holes or crevices with wood filler, sand the lamp base thoroughly, and paint or stain as desired.

8. To wire the lamp, follow the manufacturer's directions in your lamp kit. The kit will contain a threaded hollow pipe that you'll guide through holes (you'll need to drill these) in each top/bottom piece (B). Next, you'll secure the tube in place with nuts. Then you'll thread the lamp wire, with a plug at one end, through the pipe and connect it to a switch. The kit will also include spacers so that you can adjust the kit to the size of your lamp base.

Laying the Tiles

1. After the base is assembled and the wiring is in place, use paneling-and-construction adhesive to glue two ceramic tiles in place on one side (A).

2. Allow the adhesive to set up for about an hour. (You'll know the glue has set when you're unable to move the tiles with your hands.) Then repeat Step 1 three times to attach the remaining six tiles to the remaining three sides (A).

3. To raise the completed lamp from the desk surface and provide clearance for the electrical cord running from beneath the base, affix small felt or clear plastic pads to all four corners of the bottom (B) of the lamp.

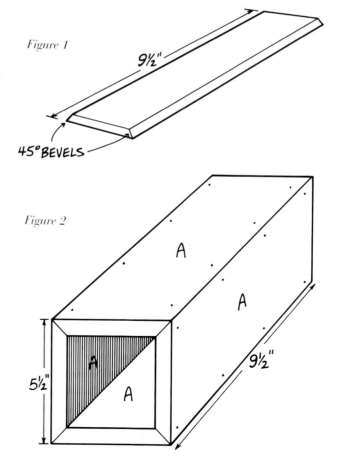

Figure 1

9½"

45° BEVELS

Figure 2

A

A

A

A

5½"

9½"

PLANTER FOR CUTTINGS

When my plants overproduce, I clip off the new growth and put it in water until it roots—a procedure which pays off in new plants, but which is also somewhat unsightly. This planter is just large enough to contain the glasses and plastic cups of water that I use for rooting and shows off the green parts of the plants without displaying the unattractive containers.

SPECIAL TOOLS AND TECHNIQUES

Bar clamps

Mitering

MATERIALS AND SUPPLIES

6 linear feet of 3/4" x 3/4" pine

10 linear feet of 1 x 6 pine

6 linear feet of 1" x 1" corner molding

HARDWARE

Approximately 25 #6 x 1-1/4" flathead wood screws

Approximately 50 3d finishing nails

CUTTING LIST

Code	Description	Qty.	Material	Dimensions
A	Side	8	1 x 6 pine	8-1/2" long
B	End	2	1 x 6 pine	8-1/2" long
C	Bottom	1	1 x 6 pine	23-1/2" long
D	Long Trim	2	3/4" x 3/4" pine	23-1/2" long
E	Short Trim	2	3/4" x 3/4" pine	7" long
F	Molding	4	1" x 1" corner molding	Cut to fit (approx. 62" total)

CONSTRUCTING THE PLANTER BOX

1. Cut ten 8-1/2"-long A and B pieces from 1 x 6 pine. For ease of instruction, we'll refer to eight of these pieces as sides (A) and two as ends (B).

2. Cut a 23-1/2"-long bottom (C) from 1 x 6 pine.

3. Position four sides (A) next to each other on a level surface, as shown in *Figure 1*.

Also place two ends (B) on edge at each end. Glue the pieces together, making certain that the assembly is perfectly square, and clamp the six pieces in place. Leave the clamp on for several hours.

4. Glue together the four remaining sides (A), as you did the previous four. Clamp these four sides together and leave the clamp in place for several hours.

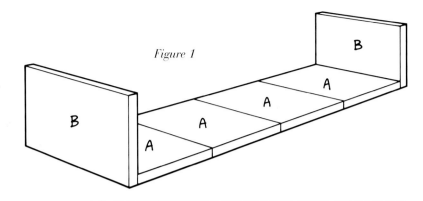

Figure 1

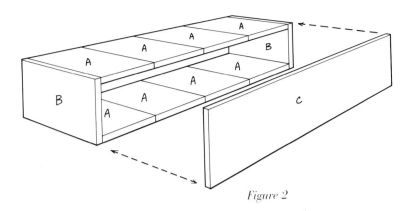

Figure 2

5. To create the long box shown in *Figure 2*, glue the four sides (A) that you assembled in Step 4 between the two ends (B) on the assembly that you constructed in Step 3.

6. Glue the bottom (C) over the exposed edges of the long box assembly, as shown in *Figure 2*. Insert two 1-1/4" screws through the bottom (C) into each of the eight sides (A) and two ends (B).

ADDING THE TRIM

1. Cut two long trim pieces (D) from 3/4" x 3/4" pine, each measuring 23-1/2" long.

2. Cut two short trim pieces (E) from 3/4" x 3/4" pine, each measuring 7" long.

3. Glue one long trim piece (D) along the bottom of the box, placing its bottom edge 5/8" from the bottom of the planter box (see *Figure 3*). Secure the long trim piece (D) in place with 3d finishing nails spaced 4" apart.

4. Repeat Step 3 to attach the other long trim piece (D) to the opposite side of the planter box.

5. Glue one short trim piece (E) to the end of the planter box so that it overlaps the ends of the long trim pieces (see *Figure 3*). Secure the short trim piece (E) with three 3d finishing nails.

6. Repeat Step 5 to attach the remaining short trim piece (E) to the opposite end of the planter box.

ADDING THE CORNER MOLDING

1. The top edges of the planter box are concealed by mitered lengths of corner molding (F). Measure and cut four pieces of molding to fit over the top of the planter box, mitering the ends to fit together exactly.

2. Glue the four mitered molding pieces (F) onto the top edges of the planter box. Then secure them with 3d finishing nails spaced about 3" apart on the longer pieces and about 2" apart on the shorter pieces.

FINISHING

1. Fill all holes, cracks, and crevices with wood filler.

2. Sand all surfaces of the planter box thoroughly.

3. Stain or paint the planter box the color of your choice. We've decorated our planter with 4" x 4" tiles. If you'd like to add tiles to yours, just turn to the instructions provided with the Tiled Lamp project on pages 32-33.

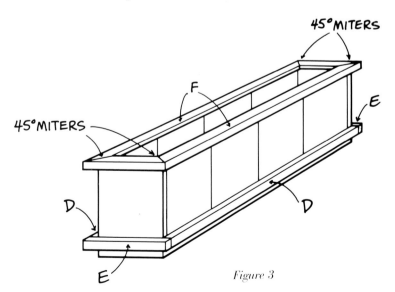

45° MITERS

45° MITERS

Figure 3

DRESSING TABLE

Most girls have lots of very important "stuff" that can't be accommodated in their dressers, and they never have enough room for displaying perfume bottles, pictures, knickknacks, and jewelry. This fabric-covered dressing table (see page 39) solves the problem. It's even large enough to double as a study desk!

MATERIALS AND SUPPLIES

22 linear feet of 1 x 8 pine

19 linear feet of 1 x 12 pine

1 piece of 1/4"-thick plywood, 30" x 48"

1 piece of 3/4"-thick plywood, 22" x 48"

1 piece of 1/8"-thick glass, 22" x 48"

1 double-layered piece of quilt batting, 26" x 52"

5-1/2 yards of 3/4"-diameter cording

2 coordinating fabrics, each 36"-wide:

    Fabric #1, 1-1/2 yards for table top

    Fabric #1, 1/2 yard for cording

    Fabric #2, 5-1/2 yards for skirt

    Fabric #2, 1/2 yard for cording

Optional extra fabric for covering back of assembly:

    Fabric #1, 1/4 yard for cording

    Fabric #2, 2-3/4 yards for skirt

    Fabric #2, 1/4 yard for cording

CUTTING LIST

Code	Description	Qty.	Material	Dimensions
A	Side	4	1 x 12 pine	28-1/2" long
B	Top/Bottom	4	1 x 12 pine	13-1/2" long
C	Shelf	4	1 x 12 pine	12" long
D	Back	2	1/4" plywood	13-1/2" x 30"
E	Bin Front/Back	12	1 x 8 pine	11-3/4" long
F	Bin Side	12	1 x 8 pine	9" long
G	Bin Bottom	6	1/4" plywood	9-3/8" x 10-5/8"
H	Table Top	1	3/4" plywood	22" x 48"

HARDWARE

Approximately 50 #6 x 1-1/4" flathead wood screws

Approximately 40 #6 x 2" flathead wood screws

Approximately 25 3d finishing nails

NOTES ON MATERIALS

Because I wanted to place my finished dressing table against a wall, I bought only enough fabric to cover its front and sides. (Okay, I'm cheap!) If you'd like to skirt the back of the dressing table, too, add the extra fabric and cording listed in the "Materials List."

Unless you want to make your own cording, purchase it from a fabric shop, coordinating it with your selected fabrics.

MAKING THE BASE UNITS

1. Underneath the skirt, the dressing table is supported by two identical units, each of which contains three drawers. To make the first unit, start by cutting the following pieces from 1 x 12 pine: two 28-1/2"-long sides (A); two 13-1/2"-long top/bottom pieces (B); and two 12"-long shelf pieces (C).

2. Glue the two top/bottom pieces (B) over the raw ends of the two sides (A) to form a rectangular box as shown in *Figure 1*. Insert three 1-1/4" screws at each joint.

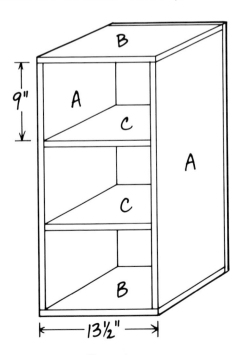

Figure 1

3. Fit the two shelves (C) into the rectangular box, spacing them evenly, so that each of the three openings is exactly 9" high (see *Figure 1*).

4. Glue the shelves (C) to the sides (A) and insert four 2" screws along the length of each joint.

5. Cut one 13-1/2" x 30" back (D) from 1/4"-thick plywood. Glue the back (D) onto the back edges of the assembled unit, as shown in *Figure 1*, and secure it with 3d finishing nails spaced 4" apart.

6. Repeat Steps 1 through 5 to construct a second base unit that is identical to the first.

Making the Drawer/Bins

1. There are a total of six bins, three in each of the dressing-table units. These aren't actually drawers, as they simply sit inside the units, but they can be pulled out if desired. Each bin is identical in size and in the method of construction (see *Figure 2*). To make them, start by cutting twelve 11-3/4"-long bin front/back pieces (E) and twelve 9"-long bin sides (F) from 1 x 8 pine.

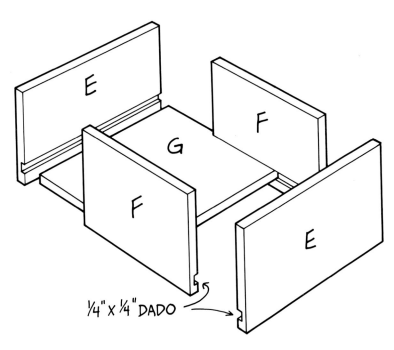

¼" x ¼" DADO

Figure 2

2. Cut a 1/4" x 1/4" dado on the inside of each bin piece (E and F), 3/8" from its lower edge, to accommodate the plywood bottom.

3. From 1/4"-thick plywood, cut six 9-3/8" x 10-5/8" bin bottoms (G).

4. Assemble and glue together one bin as shown in *Figure 2*. Note that the bin front/back pieces (E) overlap the ends of the bin sides (F). Use three 1-1/4" screws at each joint.

5. Repeat the bin-assembly process in Step 4 five more times to construct the remaining five bins.

Constructing the Top

1. The dressing table top is constructed of 3/4"-thick plywood covered with quilt batting and fabric #1. The skirt—made from fabric #2—is then attached to the table top (H). Start by cutting a 22" x 48" table top (H) from 3/4"-thick plywood.

2. Cut a 26" x 52" double layer of quilt batting.

3. Cut a 26" x 52" piece of fabric #1.

4. Place the piece of fabric #1 on a smooth surface, right side down. Place the double layer of quilt batting over the fabric. Center the top (H) over the quilt batting. Then bring the edges of the fabric up and over the edges of the table top (H) and staple them to the plywood. To minimize wrinkling, first staple the center of one side, then the center of the opposite side, and work your way out to the corners, smoothing the fabric as you go. Staple the centers of the remaining sides and again work your way out to the corners. Be generous with the staples; use enough to keep the fabric taut and eliminate puckering along the sides.

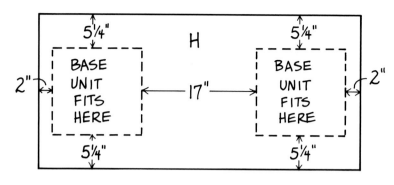

Figure 3

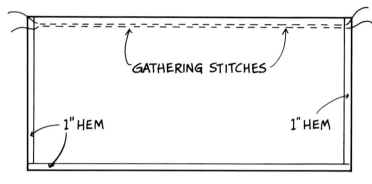

Figure 4

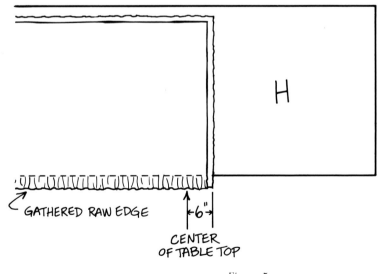

GATHERED RAW EDGE

6"

CENTER OF TABLE TOP

Figure 5

5. To attach the fabric-covered top to the two base units, place the top upside down on a flat surface. Place the two base units upside down on top of it, spacing them as shown in *Figure 3*. Attach the base units to the top by inserting 1-1/4" screws through all four corners of each of the units. Turn the entire assembly right side up when you're finished.

MAKING THE SKIRT

1. If you intend to skirt all four sides of the assembly, skip to Step 7. To skirt the two sides and front, first cut the 5-1/2-yard-long piece of fabric #2 in half to get two pieces, each 2-3/4 yards long.

2. Sew a 1" hem along the 2-3/4-yard edge of one of these two pieces and along both of the sides, as shown in *Figure 4*.

3. Sew a double row of gathering stitches 1" from the remaining raw edge (see *Figure 4*). Pull the gathers until the gathered edge measures 56".

4. Repeat Steps 2 and 3 to hem and gather the remaining 2-3/4-yard long piece of fabric #2.

5. Now you'll attach the gathered edges of these two pieces onto the edge of the padded table top (H). Place the first fabric piece right side down on the left side of the table top (H), with the gathered edge overhanging the edge of the table top and the hem 6" right of center, as shown in *Figure 5*. Adjust the overhang so that when the gathered skirt piece is stapled and pulled down, the skirt will just touch the floor. Staple the skirt to the top edge of the table top. Don't be stingy with the staples; you want a perfectly straight edge after you turn the skirt down. Work your way from 6" left of center, left across the front, across the side, and 4" around on the back.

6. Repeat Step 5 to attach the remaining piece of gathered fabric to the right side of the padded table top. The two pieces should overlap by 6" in the center of the dressing table.

7. To skirt all four sides of the entire assembly, hem and attach the entire 8-1/4 yards of fabric #2 as a single piece, beginning and ending with a 6" overlap in the front.

ADDING THE CORDING

1. Now you'll cover the edge of the skirt cording with fabric #1. Because the fabric will be gathered, it must be twice as long as the cording itself. Start by cutting the 5-1/2 yards of cording in half so that you have two equal pieces, each 2-3/4 yards long.

2. Using the 1/2 yard of fabric #1, cut and seam together enough 3"-wide x 36"-long strips to produce a strip 3" wide and 5-1/2 yards long.

3. Fold the fabric strip lengthwise and sew a 1/2" seam along the raw edges.

4. Turn the fabric strip right side out to form a tube.

5. Pull one piece of the cording through the tube and adjust the gathers evenly along the length.

6. Repeat Steps 2 through 5 to cover the remaining cording with the 1/2 yard of fabric #2.

7. Glue the cording covered with fabric #1 to the top edge of the padded table top (H), over the gathered skirt. Begin at the back, work across one side, across the front, across the other side, and end at the back.

8. Repeat Step 7 to glue the cording covered with fabric #2 just below the previously glued cording.

9. Set the piece of 1/4" glass on top of your finished dressing table and await the rave reviews!

BATHROOM WALL RACK

Does anyone ever have enough shelf space in the bathroom? This project is one solution to the problem of where to store towels, magazines, perfume bottles, and other items you need within reach. It's easy to build, and you can paint the finished project to pick up the colors of your bathroom.

SPECIAL TECHNIQUES

Ripping

MATERIALS AND SUPPLIES

4 linear feet of 1 x 2 pine

13 linear feet of 1 x 6 pine

5 linear feet of 1 x 8 pine

HARDWARE

Approximately 20 #6 x 1-1/4" flathead wood screws

Approximately 25 #6 x 1-1/2" flathead wood screws

CUTTING LIST

Code	Description	Qty.	Material	Dimensions
A	Shelf	4	1 x 6 pine	20-3/4" long
B	Divider	1	1 x 6 pine	8-1/2" long
C	Side	2	1 x 6 pine	29-1-2" long
D	Rail	2	1 x 2 pine	20-3/4" long
E	Top/Bottom	2	1 x 8 pine, ripped	24-1/4" long

MAKING THE BASIC FRAME

1. Cut four 20-3/4"-long shelves (A) from 1 x 6 pine.

2. Cut one 8-1/2"-long divider (B) from 1 x 6 pine.

3. Position two of the shelves (A) on a level surface, parallel to each other and 8-1/2" apart. Position the divider (B) between the two shelves (A), locating its ends in the exact center of each shelf (see *Figure 1*). Glue the divider (B) in place and insert two 1-1/2" screws through each of the shelves (A) and into the divider (B).

4. Cut two sides (C) from 1 x 6 pine, each 29-1/2" long.

5. Place the divider/shelf assembly (see Step 3) on a level surface. Place a third shelf (A) parallel to the divider/shelf assembly and 8" above it, as shown in *Figure 2*. Position the remaining shelf (A) parallel to the divider/shelf assembly and 10" below it. Position the two sides (C) along the sides of the assembly and the third and fourth shelves (A). Glue the sides (C) to the edges of the shelves (A) and insert two 1-1/2" screws through each side (C) and into the ends of each shelf (A).

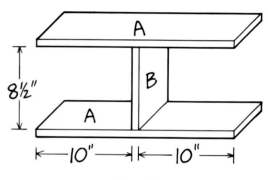

Figure 1

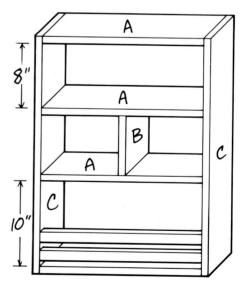

Figure 2

Adding the Rails

1. Cut two 20-3/4"-long rails (D) from 1 x 2 pine.

2. Glue one rail (D) between the two sides (C), 1/2" above the bottom shelf (A), as shown in *Figure 3*. Secure the rail by inserting a 1-1/4" screw through each side (C) and into each end of the rail (D).

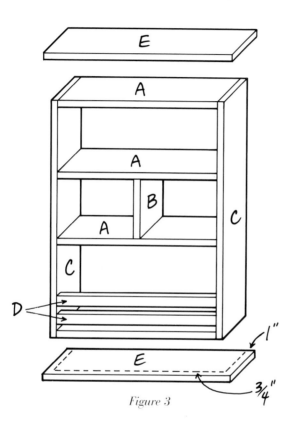

Figure 3

3. Repeat Step 2 to attach the second rail (D), leaving 3/4" between its lower edge and the upper edge of the first rail (see *Figure 3*).

Adding the Top and Bottom

1. Rip 5 linear feet of 1 x 8 pine to a width of 6-1/4".

2. Cut two 24-1/4"-long top/bottom pieces (E) from the ripped pine.

3. To attach one top/bottom piece (E) to the top of the shelf assembly, first center the top/bottom piece over the assembly so that there is a 1" overhang at each end (see *Figure 3*). Because the completed rack must hang on the wall, the back of

the top/bottom piece (E) should be flush with the back of the shelf assembly and should overhang by 3/4" in front. Glue the top/bottom piece (E) in place and use four 1-1/4" screws to attach it to the top shelf (A), centering the screws along the length of the board and spacing them evenly.

4. Repeat Step 3 to attach the remaining top/bottom piece (E) to the bottom of the shelf assembly.

Finishing

1. Fill all holes, cracks, and crevices with wood filler.

2. Sand all surfaces of the completed shelf thoroughly.

3. Paint or stain the shelf with colors of your choice.

TRIANGULAR TABLE

Every so often a very easy project turns out to be an all-time favorite. That's the case with this small triangular table (see page 46). Although it takes almost no time to put together, I've received more than my share of "attaboys" for the finished product. I wanted a triangular table to fit next to my couch, which is positioned diagonally in my family room. Here's the result!

SPECIAL TECHNIQUES

Mitering

MATERIALS AND SUPPLIES

8 linear feet of 1 x 4 pine

6 linear feet of 4 x 4 pine

1 piece of 3/4" plywood, 24" x 24"

3 fence finials

HARDWARE

Approximately 50 #6 x 1-1/4" flathead wood screws

CUTTING LIST

Code	Description	Qty.	Material	Dimensions
A	Top	1	3/4" plywood	See *Fig. 1*
B	Short Trim	1	1 x 4 pine	25-1/2" long
C	Medium Trim	1	1 x 4 pine	26-1/2" long
D	Long Trim	1	1 x 4 pine	37-1/2" long
E	Leg	3	4 x 4 pine	Cut to fit (approx. 72" total)

NOTES ON MATERIALS

We made the legs on this table by purchasing screw-in finials (sold at building-supply stores as decorative additions for porch posts) and inserting them into lengths of 4 x 4 pine. Our finials are approximately 4-1/2" long and 3" in diameter.

MAKING THE TABLE TOP

1. Using *Figure 1* as a guide, cut one triangular top (A) from 3/4"-thick plywood. The simplest way to do this is to start by marking off a 24" square on the plywood. Then draw a line to connect either set of opposite corners. Cut along the lines, and your triangle is complete.

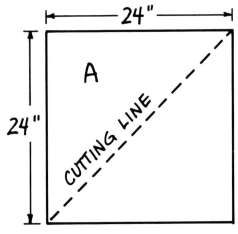

Figure 1

2. Cut one short trim piece (B) from 1 x 4 pine, measuring 25-1/2" long.

3. Miter one end of the short trim piece (B) at a 45-degree angle, as shown in *Figure 2*.

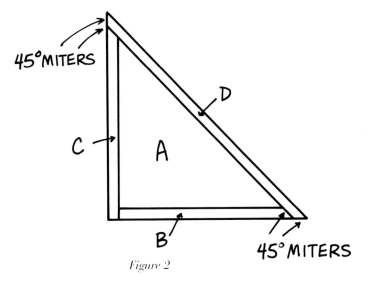

Figure 2

4. To add the short trim piece (B) to the outer edge of the top (A), first place the top upside down on a level surface. Glue the

short trim piece (B), on edge, to a 24"-long edge of the top (A) and secure it by driving 1-1/4" screws, spaced about 6" apart, through the trim (B) and into the edge of the plywood.

5. Cut one 26-1/2"-long medium trim piece (C) from 1 x 4 pine.

6. Miter one end of the medium trim piece (C) at a 45-degree angle, as shown in *Figure 2*. Note that the medium trim piece (C) overlaps the short trim piece (B) at the 90-degree corner.

7. Attach the medium trim piece (C) to the top (A), in the same way that you attached the short trim piece. Use two additional screws to connect the two trim pieces at the 90-degree corner.

8. Cut one long trim piece (D) from 1 x 4 pine, measuring 37-1/2" in length.

9. Miter both ends of the long trim piece (D) at 45-degree angles. Before attaching it, check to make certain that this piece fits perfectly along the long edge of the top (A).

10. Attach the long trim piece (D) to the top (A) in the same way that you attached the other two trim pieces. Then insert four additional 1-1/4" screws to secure the long trim piece to the other two trim pieces (B and C).

Adding the Legs

1. The legs are made by attaching decorative finials to the ends of pine 4 x 4s (E). To find the bottom center of each 4 x 4, simply draw two lines to connect the opposing corners at one end (see *Figure 3*). The point at which the two lines intersect is the center. Apply glue to the meeting surfaces of the 4 x 4 and one finial; then hand-screw the finial into the marked center of the 4 x 4.

2. Measure and mark a point 25" from the end of the finial down the leg (E). Cut the leg to this length.

3. Repeat Steps 1 and 2 to make two more legs (E).

4. Using *Figure 4* as a placement guide, glue the three legs (E) to the bottom face of the top (A). To secure the legs, first insert two 1-1/4" screws through each abutting

trim piece (B, C, and D) and into each leg. Also insert four 1-1/4" screws through the top (A) and into the end of each leg, positioning the screws at the corners of the legs, but not so close to the corners that you split the wood.

Finishing

1. Fill all holes, cracks, and crevices with wood filler.

2. Sand the entire table thoroughly.

3. Paint or stain the finished table the color of your choice. We decided to sponge-paint our table to simulate the plaid in our furniture. Although doing this looks difficult, it's actually quite easy. Start by painting the table with the base color of your choice. Next, sponge-paint stripes in one direction and let them dry. Then sponge-paint stripes in the opposite direction. We were really pleased with the results.

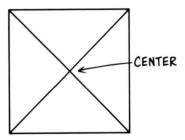

Figure 3

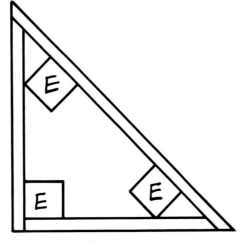

Figure 4

Upholstered Ottoman

This ottoman is an extremely versatile piece of furniture. As well as using it as a regular ottoman, I've placed a tray on top of it and used it as a table between two chairs and have also used it as extra seating. The project is fairly easy to make and inexpensive to build.

Special Techniques

Mitering

Materials and Supplies

5 linear feet of 3/4" x 3/4" pine

22 linear feet of 1 x 4 pine

1 piece of 3/4"-thick plywood, 16-1/2" x 16-1/2"

1 piece of 2"-thick foam rubber, 17" x 17"

3 yards of decorative fabric, 36" wide

Hardware

Approximately 150 #6 x 1-1/4" flathead wood screws

Approximately 10 #6 x 2-1/2" flathead wood screws

Cutting List

Code	Description	Qty.	Material	Dimensions
A	Leg	8	1 x 4 pine	16" long
B	Front/Back Connector	2	1 x 4 pine	14" long
C	Side Connector	2	1 x 4 pine	15-1/2" long
D	Front/Back Spacer	2	1 x 4 pine	8-1/2" long
E	Side Spacer	2	1 x 4 pine	10" long
F	Corner Support	4	1 x 4 pine	8-1/2" long
G	Leg Support	4	3/4" x 3/4" pine	12-1/2" long
H	Seat Bottom	1	3/4" plywood	16-1/2" x 16-1/2"

Cutting and Assembly

1. Cut all the wooden parts in the "Cutting List," and label each one with its code letter.

2. The seat frame consists of two side assemblies, a front assembly, and a back assembly. All of the components should be fastened together with both wood glue and screws, and each assembly should be checked carefully to make sure that the joints are perfectly square.

The construction of these assemblies is shown in *Figure 1*. Start by positioning one side connector (C) on two legs (A), spacing the pieces as shown in the illustration. The upper edge of the side connector (C) should be flush with the ends of the legs (A), and there should be a 3/4" offset at each end of the side connector (C). Fasten the parts together using glue and two 1-1/4" screws at each end of the side connector (C) to attach it to the legs (A).

3. Glue the side spacer (E) between the legs (A), as shown in *Figure 1*. Drive three 1-1/4" screws through the side connector (C) and into the side spacer (E).

4. Repeat Steps 2 and 3 to construct the second side assembly.

5. The front assembly is assembled in the same fashion (see *Figure 1*). Assemble two legs (A) and one front/back connector (B), spacing the parts as shown. Again, the pieces should be flush at the top, and there should be a 3/4" offset at the ends of the connector (B). To secure the legs (A), use glue and two 1-1/4" screws at each end of the front/back connector (B). Attach the front/back spacer (D) between the legs (A), using three 1-1/4" screws driven through the front/back connector (B) and into the front/back spacer (D).

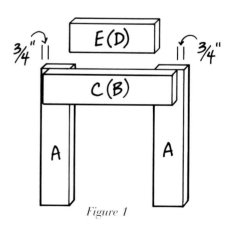

Figure 1

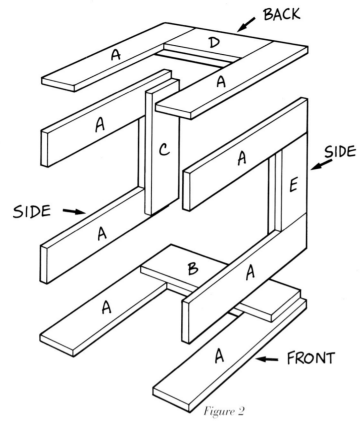

BACK

SIDE

SIDE

FRONT

Figure 2

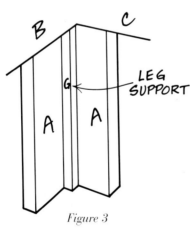

LEG
SUPPORT

Figure 3

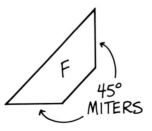

45°
MITERS

Figure 4

6. Repeat Step 5 to make the identical back assembly.

7. Attach the two side assemblies to the front and back assemblies as shown in *Figure 2*, making certain that the legs (A) are flush at both the top and bottom. Note that the side assemblies overlap the exposed ends of the front and back assemblies. Apply glue to the meeting edges and insert 1-1/4" screws, spacing them about 5" apart along the joints at the legs (A).

8. Cut four 12-1/2"-long leg supports (G) from 3/4" x 3/4" pine. Glue one leg support (G) to the inside corner of each of the four leg assemblies (see *Figure 3*) and insert three or four 1-1/4" screws through each of the exposed sides of the leg supports (G) and into the legs (A) behind them.

9. Set each corner support (F) on its face and miter each end at a 45-degree angle, as shown in *Figure 4*.

10. Using *Figure 5* as a placement guide, position the mitered corner supports (F), making certain that their faces are flush with the top edges of the assembled frame. Glue the corner supports (F) in place and insert 2-1/2" screws through the edges of each one, driving the screws at an angle into the front, back, and side connectors (B and C).

11. Patch any crevices or gaps in the completed frame with wood putty; then sand the frame thoroughly.

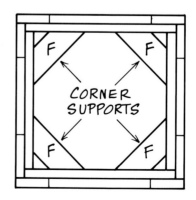

CORNER
SUPPORTS

Figure 5

12. Because the entire ottoman will be covered with fabric, you needn't stain or paint the wooden portions. If you'd like to, however, now is the time.

ADDING THE SKIRT

1. Cut four 19" lengths of 36"-wide fabric. Seam the four widths together along their 19"-long edges to form a long rectangular piece of fabric, as shown in *Figure 6*.

2. Sew a 1"-wide hem along one long edge of the seamed fabric and along both 19"-long ends.

3. Fold the long fabric strip in half across its 19" width to find its center. Mark the center point with a pin. Fold the fabric in half across its width again and mark each of the half-points with a pin. Unfold the fabric and hold the center point of the raw edge onto the top surface of the ottoman assembly at the center front (see *Figure 7*). This is the time to decide how long you want the fabric skirt to be. I let mine drape on the floor, but you can attach the raw edge to allow for whatever skirt length you prefer. Just be sure to keep the length equal on all sides of the ottoman. Staple the fabric at the center front to the top of the ottoman assembly. Then staple each of the half-points to the top of the ottoman assembly at the center sides. Overlap the two hemmed ends and staple them to the center back.

4. Working from the center back out to the two nearest corners, smooth and staple the fabric to the top of the ottoman assembly. Repeat this procedure, working from each of the stapled center and half-points out to the corners. You will now have excess fabric at each corner.

5. Form the excess fabric into a giant pleat at each corner (see *Figure 7*) and staple the pleat to the top of the ottoman frame.

MAKING THE SEAT CUSHION

1. Center the 17"-square piece of foam rubber over the 16-1/2"-square plywood seat bottom (H) and glue it in place.

2. Center the remaining 32" x 36" piece of fabric over the foam rubber and wrap the fabric over the edges of the seat bottom (H). To minimize wrinkles as you staple the fabric to the underside of the seat bottom (H), first staple the center of one side, then the center of the opposite side, and then work your way out to the corners, smoothing the fabric as you go. Staple the centers of the remaining sides and again work your way out to the corners. Be generous with the staples; use enough to keep the fabric from puckering along the sides.

3. To attach the upholstered seat cushion to the frame, place the seat cushion upside down on a flat surface and place the frame upside down on top of it. Insert two or three 1-1/4" screws through each of the corner supports (F) and into the seat bottom (H).

4. Place the completed ottoman right side up and have a seat!

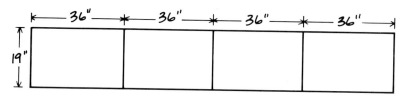

Figure 6

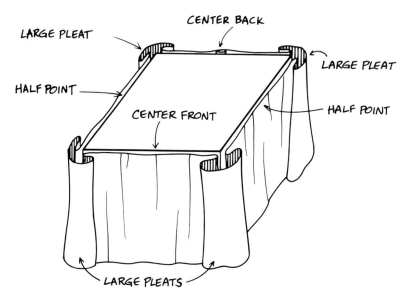

Figure 7

51

Padded Headboard

*Here's an inexpensive and easy way to make
a decorator headboard for your bed.
Although we made ours for a queen-size bed,
you can alter the dimensions to fit any bed
from twin to king-size. We used two coordinating fabrics to match our duvet cover and
bed pillows. The headboard shown in the
photo, by the way, was customized to fit a
waterbed with an existing wooden frame.
It's just slightly different from the project
described here, which is designed to fit a
standard metal bed frame.*

Special Tools

Staple gun and 5/8" staples

Saber saw

Materials and Supplies

1 sheet of 3/4"-thick plywood, 4' x 8'

1 piece of 2"-thick foam rubber, 2' x 5'

6 bags of polyester fiberfill

2 yards of 36"-wide decorator fabric

3-1/2 yards of 36"-wide coordinating fabric

2 yards of 36"-wide backing fabric (optional)

Decorative cording (optional)

Hardware

2 large bolts with matching nuts, 1-1/2" long

Cutting List

Code	Description	Qty.	Material	Dimensions
A	Headboard	1	3/4" plywood	48" x 65"

Notes on Materials

Standard metal frames come with holes in the
metal brackets at the head of the bed; the holes
accommodate the bolts with which you'll attach
the leg portions of your headboard, so be sure to
check the hole size before purchasing bolts.

Buy the cheapest plywood you can find; it will be
covered with fabric, so its flaws will be invisible.

Because we wanted to stack pillows against the
completed project, we made it taller than most
headboards. Feel free to alter the specific dimensions to please your own taste.

To make certain that our headboard dimensions
will fit your bed (see *Figure 1*), we suggest that you
cut a trial headboard shape out of heavy paper
and tape it to the wall behind your bed. When
you're certain you're pleased with the result, use
the paper as a pattern for marking and cutting the
plywood.

Cutting the Plywood

1. Cut out the plywood headboard first
(see *Figure 1*), leaving the top corners
square. To round the corners, place any
circular object (a round tray works well) on
each upper corner, trace around it, and
then follow the traced lines with your saber
saw.

2. Measure 6" in from the edges of the plywood headboard (A) and draw a rough
stapling line, as shown in *Figure 1*.

3. Using *Figure 1* as a guide, cut one piece
of 2"-thick foam rubber to cover the upper
portion of the headboard. The foam
shouldn't extend all the way to the stapling
line; leave about 1-1/2" between that line
and the cut edge of the foam.

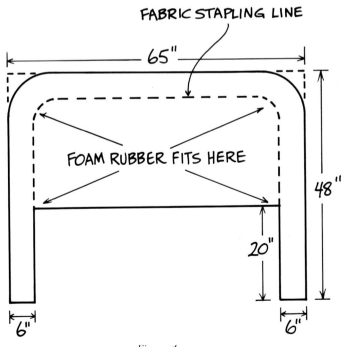

Figure 1

4. Place the foam on the plywood headboard (A) and staple it in place along the stapling line by bending its upper edges down to meet the line, as shown in *Figure 2*. Staple the foam at the bottom of the headboard, too.

ADDING THE FABRIC

1. Cut one piece of 36"-wide decorator fabric large enough to cover all of the foam rubber and to overlap it by 2" on all edges.

2. Staple the decorator fabric over the foam rubber, placing the staples along the fabric stapling line.

3. To pad and cover the bare portions of plywood, first measure along the entire length of the stapling line and multiply the result by 2-1/2. Seam together enough 15" lengths of 36"-wide coordinating fabric to obtain that result. (Be sure to seam the 15" edges together.)

4. Sew gathering stitches along one long edge of the seamed-together lengths. Pull the gathering stitches until the gathered edge is the same length as the stapling line.

5. Place the gathered edge right-side down, matching the gathering line and the stapling line. Let the fabric drape over the padded portion of the headboard. Then staple the gathered coordinated fabric to the stapling line. Don't be stingy with the staples—they should form an almost a solid line.

6. Now you'll pad the top portion of the headboard as you bring the stapled fabric up over it; you'll need to experiment to get just the right amount of fiberfill and to distribute it evenly over the top of the headboard. Beginning at one side of the headboard, cover a 2' section of the 6"-wide exposed wood and the edge of the plywood headboard with a generous amount

of fiberfill. Then pull the gathered fabric up over the fiberfill and the edge of the headboard. (This will be easier if you can find a helper to hold the fabric in place while you evaluate your work.) Adjust the amount of fiberfill, if necessary. When you're satisfied with the way the headboard looks, staple the other edge of the fabric to the back of the headboard (A), adjusting the gathers evenly along the 2' section of the headboard.

7. Repeat this procedure to pad the remaining portion of the headboard, working in 2' sections all the way around.

8. Next, you'll cover the leg portions of the plywood. Cut two pieces of decorator fabric 2" wider than these leg portions.

9. Cover the front of one leg portion with one piece, turning under 1/2"-wide seams at the top and bottom edges of the fabric. Wrap the fabric around to the back of the plywood and staple it in place.

10. Repeat Step 9 to cover the front and edges of the remaining leg with fabric.

11. If you wish to finish the back of the headboard, simply cut a piece of backing fabric 2" larger than the headboard on all sides, turn under a 2"-wide hem, and staple the fabric to the back of the headboard. Cover the staples with decorative cording.

FINISHING

1. Place the finished headboard behind the bed and align the legs with the metal brackets on the bed frame. Mark the position of the bed-frame holes on the headboard legs.

2. Drill holes through the headboard legs large enough to accommodate the bolts you've purchased. Insert the bolts through the headboard and through the holes in the metal bed frame. Tighten the nuts on the bolts.

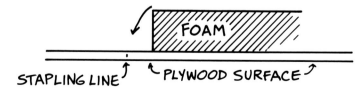

Figure 2

BUTLER'S CHEST

Because it's designed to suit a variety of purposes, this butler's chest (see page 56) is a piece of furniture that absolutely anyone can appreciate. Used by itself, it can serve as an end table or can be fit under a window. Two chests placed back-to-back form a great-looking coffee table. For extra storage space, you can even stack two or three chests on top of one another.

SPECIAL TECHNIQUES

Beveling

Mitering

MATERIALS AND SUPPLIES

9 linear feet of 1 x 3 pine

10 linear feet of 1 x 4 pine

16 linear feet of 2 x 4 pine

1 piece of 1/4"-thick plywood, 14" x 25"

1 sheet of 3/4"-thick plywood, 4' x 8'

20 linear feet of 3/4"-wide decorative molding

HARDWARE

Approximately 20 #6 x 3/4" flathead wood screws

Approximately 100 #6 x 1-1/4" flathead wood screws

Approximately 20 #6 x 2" flathead wood screws

Approximately 20 #6 x 2-1/2" flathead wood screws

Approximately 30 wire brads

4 offset door hinges

2 decorative cabinet-door pulls

CUTTING LIST

Code	Description	Qty.	Material	Dimensions
A	Long Inner Support	4	2 x 4 pine	34-1/2" long
B	Short Inner Support	4	2 x 4 pine	12-1/2" long
C	Side	2	3/4" plywood	16-1/4" x 20-1/2"
D	Back	1	3/4" plywood	20-1/2" x 36"
E	Vertical Trim	3	1 x 4 pine	20-1/2" long
F	Horizontal Trim	4	1 x 4 pine	12-3/4" long
G	Top/Bottom	2	3/4" plywood	18" x 38"
H	Cabinet Door	2	1/4" plywood	12-1/4" x 13"
I	Top/Bottom Trim	4	1 x 3 pine	14-1/4" long
J	Side Trim	4	1 x 3 pine	10" long

MAKING THE INNER FRAME

1. The inner frame of the butler's chest, which is covered with 3/4"-thick plywood, consists of two rectangular inner support assemblies connected to each other by two sides and a back. Start by cutting four long inner supports (A) from 2 x 4 pine, each measuring 34-1/2" long.

2. Cut four short inner supports (B) from 2 x 4 pine, each measuring 12-1/2" long.

3. Place two long inner supports (A) on a level surface, parallel to each other, on edge, and 12-1/2" apart. Fit two short inner supports (B) between the two long inner supports (A), as shown in *Figure 1*. Glue the supports together and insert two 2-1/2" screws through the long inner supports (A) into the ends of the short inner supports (B) at each joint. You now have one inner support assembly.

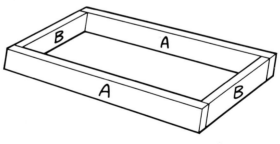

Figure 1

4. Repeat Step 3, using the remaining two short inner supports (B) and two long inner supports (A) to construct a second inner support assembly.

ADDING THE SIDES AND BACK

1. Cut two 16-1/4" x 20-1/2" sides (C) from 3/4"-thick plywood.

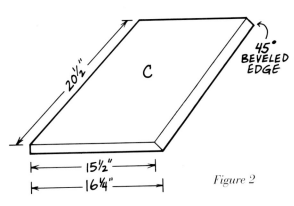

2. Bevel one 20-1/2"-long edge of each side (C) at a 45-degree angle, as shown in *Figure 2*.

3. Glue one side (C) to the two inner support assemblies, as shown in *Figure 3*. Note that the two assemblies fit flush with the 15-1/2"-long, non-beveled edge of the side (C) and that the beveled portion of the side (C) extends past the assemblies. Secure with 2" screws inserted through the side (C) and into each of the assemblies; space the screws about 4" apart.

Figure 2

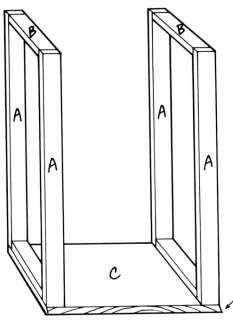

Figure 3

4. Attach the third vertical trim piece (E) in the center of the cabinet, as shown in *Figure 5*, inserting two 1-1/4" screws through the top and bottom of the vertical trim piece (E) into the long inner supports (A) at each joint. Note that the spacing between the vertical trim pieces (E) should be exactly 12-3/4".

5. Cut four 12-3/4"-long horizontal trim pieces (F) from 1 x 4 pine.

6. Using *Figure 5* as a guide, glue the four horizontal trim pieces (F) flush with the top and bottom of the cabinet, between the

4. Repeat Step 3 to attach the remaining side (C) to the opposite side of the inner support assemblies.

5. Cut one 20-1/2" x 36" back (D) from 3/4"-thick plywood.

6. Bevel each of the 20-1/2"-long edges of the back (D) at a 45-degree angle, in the same manner that you did on one edge of each side (C).

7. Glue the back (D) over the beveled edges of the sides (C), matching the bevels as shown in *Figure 4*. Insert 1-1/4" screws, spaced about 6" apart, through the back (D) and into both of the long inner supports (A).

ADDING THE FRONT TRIM

1. Cut three 20-1/2"-long vertical trim pieces (E) from 1 x 4 pine.

2. Glue one vertical trim piece (E) to the left side of the cabinet, as shown in *Figure 5*, and insert 1-1/4" screws, spaced about 6" apart, through the vertical trim piece (E) and into the long inner supports (A) and the edge of the side (C).

3. Repeat Step 2 to attach a second vertical trim piece (E) to the right side of the cabinet.

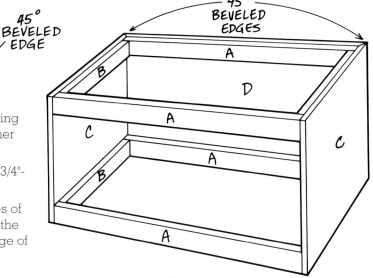

Figure 4

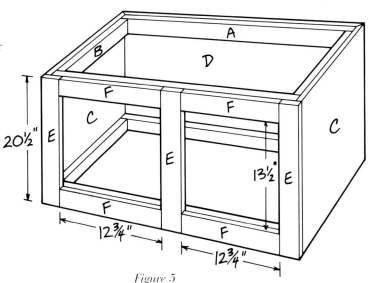

Figure 5

vertical trim pieces (E). Secure with three 1-1/4" screws driven through each of the four horizontal trim pieces (F). Note that the opening between the top and bottom horizontal trim pieces (F) should be exactly 12-3/4" x 13-1/2".

ADDING THE TOP AND BOTTOM

1. Cut two 18" x 38" top/bottom pieces (G) from 3/4"-thick plywood.

2. Center one top/bottom (G) over the cabinet assembly so that it's flush with the edge of the back (D) and overhangs by 1" at the front and at each side. Glue the top/bottom (G) in place and insert 1-1/4" screws through it and into the inner support assemblies, spacing the screws about 6" apart.

3. Turn the cabinet upside-down and repeat Step 2 to attach the remaining top/bottom (G) to it.

4. To cover the exposed edges and ends of the plywood top/bottom pieces (G), cut and fit 3/4"-wide decorative molding, mitering the molding at the corners. Glue the molding in place and secure with wire brads spaced about 6" apart.

MAKING THE CABINET DOORS

1. The cabinet doors are nothing more than pieces of 1/4"-thick plywood trimmed with borders of 1 x 3 pine. They're easy to make, but do be certain that the finished doors are perfectly square. Start by cutting two 12-1/4" x 13" cabinet door pieces (H) from 1/4"-thick plywood.

2. Cut four 14-1/4" long top/bottom trim pieces (I) from 1 x 3 pine.

3. Cut four side trim pieces (J) from 1 x 3 pine, each measuring 10" long.

4. Place two top/bottom trim pieces (I) and two side trim pieces (J) on a level surface, as shown in *Figure 6*. Center the cabinet door (H) over the trim pieces. There should be a 1"-wide border of trim visible along each of the four edges of the cabinet door (H). Glue the pieces together and insert 3/4" screws through the door (H) and into the trim pieces, spacing the screws about 4" apart.

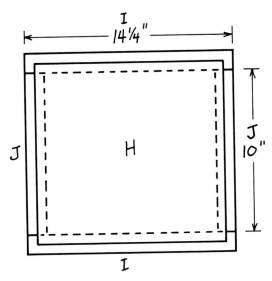

Figure 6

5. Repeat Step 4 to assemble the second cabinet door.

FINISHING

1. Fill any cracks, crevices, or holes with wood filler.

2. Sand all surfaces thoroughly.

3. Paint or stain the cabinet and doors the color of your choice.

4. Install the hinges on each of the doors, first measuring carefully to ensure that the hinges are positioned the same distance from the top and bottom of each door.

5. Have someone help you support the doors while you hold them over the door openings. Line up each door evenly with the door next to it and make sure that neither door scrapes any surface of its opening. Then attach the remaining sides of the hinges to the cabinet.

6. Attach the pulls to each of the cabinet doors, spacing them evenly and aligning them with each other.

WALL CABINET

I built this cabinet (see page 60) for my kitchen to provide both storage and visual interest on a very blank wall. I saved space—and materials—by allowing the wall to serve as the cabinet's back. The project is built in sections and then attached to the wall. The center shelves can be altered in length to fit just about any space you wish. If you have a smaller wall (perhaps in a bathroom), build only one of the end cabinets.

MATERIALS AND SUPPLIES

24 linear feet of 1 x 3 pine
63 linear feet of 1 x 4 pine
50 linear feet of 1 x 6 pine
4 shutter doors, each measuring 15-1/4" x 23"

HARDWARE

Approximately 150 #6 x 1-1/4" screws
Approximately 50 3d finishing nails
4 door latches
4 decorative door pulls
8 flush-mounted hinges
18 molly bolts (or other appropriate hardware to attach the project to the wall)

CUTTING LIST

Code	Description	Qty.	Material	Dimensions
A	Top/Bottom	4	1 x 6 pine	37-1/2" long
B	Side	4	1 x 6 pine	28-1/2" long
C	Shelf	4	1 x 6 pine	36" long
D	Vertical Trim	4	1 x 4 pine	30" long
E	Center Vertical Support	2	1 x 4 pine	28-1/2" long
F	Horizontal Trim	4	1 x 4 pine	30-1/2" long
G	Long Base	4	1 x 4 pine	30" long
H	Short Base	4	1 x 4 pine	3-1/2" long
I	Base Top	2	1 x 4 pine	31-1/2" long
J	Center Shelf	3	1 x 6 pine	58" long
K	Center Shelf Trim	3	1 x 4 pine	58" long
L	Side Support	6	1 x 3 pine	5-1/2" long
M	Back Support	3	1 x 3 pine	56-1/2" long
N	Wall Support	2	1 x 3 pine	32" long

NOTES ON MATERIALS

To save time and to avoid having to build cabinet doors, I purchased pre-made shutter doors, which are available at most building-supply stores. If you can't find shutters in the specified size, it's usually possible to cut them down to fit. If all else fails, simply alter the dimensions of the cabinet to accommodate the shutters you find.

MAKING THE CABINET FRAME

1. Cut four 37-1/2"-long top/bottom pieces (A) from 1 x 6 pine.

2. Cut four 28-1/2"-long side pieces (B) from 1 x 6 pine.

3. Place two of the top/bottom pieces (A) on a level surface, on edge, parallel to each other, and 28-1/2" apart. Fit two of the side pieces (B) between the ends of the top/bottom pieces (A), as shown in *Figure 1*. Glue the pieces together and insert three 1-1/4" screws through the top/bottom pieces (A) into the ends of the sides (B) at each joint.

4. Cut four 36"-long shelves (C) from 1 x 6 pine.

5. A slot must be cut into each of the four shelves (C) at the center front to accommodate the center vertical support (E).

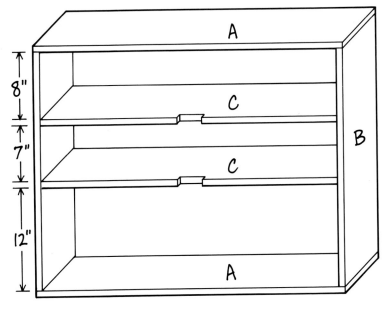

Figure 1

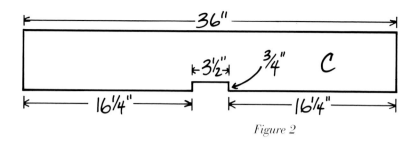

Figure 2

Using *Figure 2* as a guide, cut a slot 3-1/2" wide and 3/4" deep in the center front of each shelf (C).

6. Use 1-1/4" screws and glue to attach two of the shelves (C) inside the assembly, spacing shelves as desired. *Figure 1* shows the spacing that I chose for mine.

7. Repeat Steps 3 through 6 to construct a second cabinet frame using the remaining two top/bottom pieces (A), two sides (B), and two shelves (C).

ADDING THE TRIM
1. Cut four vertical trim pieces (D) from 1 x 4 pine, each measuring 30" long.

2. Glue one vertical trim piece (D) to the left side of the cabinet, as shown in *Figure 3*, and secure it with 1-1/4" screws inserted through the vertical trim piece (D) and into the edge of the side (B). Space the screws about 6" apart.

3. Repeat Step 2 to attach a second vertical trim piece (D) to the right side of the cabinet, as shown in *Figure 3*.

4. Cut two 28-1/2"-long center vertical supports (E) from 1 x 4 pine.

5. Fit one center vertical support (E) into the slots in the center front of the shelves (C), as shown in *Figure 3*. Glue the support in place and insert two 1-1/4" screws through the top/bottom (A) and into the end of the center vertical support (E) at each joint. Then drive two 3d finishing nails through the center vertical support (E) and into the slot in the center front of each shelf (C). Note that the spacing between the vertical pieces (D and E) should be exactly 13-1/2".

6. Cut four 30-1/2"-long horizontal trim pieces (F) from 1 x 4 pine.

7. Glue two of the horizontal trim pieces (F) flush with the top and bottom of the cabinet, between the vertical trim pieces (D), as shown in *Figure 3*. Then insert three 1-1/4" screws along each horizontal trim piece (F) to secure it to the edge of the top/bottom piece (A). Note that the opening between the top and bottom horizontal trim pieces (F) should be exactly 23".

8. Repeat Steps 1 through 7 to attach two vertical trim pieces (D), one center vertical support (E) and two horizontal trim pieces (F) to the remaining cabinet frame.

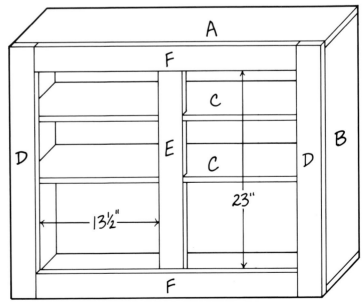

Figure 3

CONSTRUCTING THE CABINET BASE

1. To stabilize the cabinet and lift it off of the floor, we built very simple base units and attached them to the bottoms of the two assembled cabinets. Cut two long bases (G) from 1 x 4 pine, each measuring 30" long.

2. Cut two short bases (H) from 1 x 4 pine, each measuring 3-1/2" long.

3. Cut one 31-1/2" long base top (I) from 1 x 4 pine.

4. Place the two long bases (G) on a level surface, parallel to each other, on edge, and 2" apart. Glue the two short bases (H) to the ends of the two long bases (G), as shown in *Figure 4*, and insert two 1-1/4" screws through the short bases (H) and into the ends of the long bases (G) at each joint. You should end up with a rectangular base frame measuring 31-1/2" x 3-1/2".

5. Glue the base top (I) to the top edges of the base frame, as shown in *Figure 4*. Then drive 3d finishing nails through the base top (I) and into the edges of the base frame, spacing the nails about 4" apart.

6. Turn the cabinet upside down and place the completed base on its bottom, with the base top (I) against the cabinet bottom. Position the base so that the cabinet overlaps it by 2-3/4" in the front and by 3" on each side. Note that the rear of the base should be flush with the back edge of the cabinet bottom.

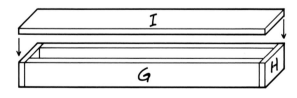

Figure 4

7. Repeat Steps 1 through 6 to build and attach a second cabinet base to the remaining cabinet.

CONSTRUCTING THE CENTER SHELVES

1. The center shelves are constructed separately and then attached to the wall between the assembled cabinets. Each shelf unit is constructed in an identical manner. Our completed shelf units measure 58" long, but you can adjust them to the exact length that you require between your two cabinets. Cut three 58"-long center shelves (J) from 1 x 6 pine.

2. Cut three 58"-long center shelf trim pieces (K) from 1 x 4 pine.

3. Cut six 5-1/2"-long side support pieces (L) from 1 x 3 pine.

4. Cut three 56-1/2"-long back support pieces (M) from 1 x 3 pine.

5. Place one center shelf piece (J) on a level surface and glue one shelf trim piece (K) onto it, flush with one long edge, as shown in *Figure 5*. Insert 1-1/4" screws, spaced approximately 6" apart, through the center shelf trim (K) and into the edge of the center shelf (J).

6. Glue the side support pieces (L) so that their outer faces are flush with the ends of the center shelf (J), as shown in *Figure 5*. Note that the center shelf trim (K) overlaps the ends of the side supports (L) and that the side supports (L) are narrower than the center shelf trim (K). Insert two 1-1/4" screws through the center shelf (J) into the edge of each side support (L).

7. Glue one back support (M) to the remaining long edge of the center shelf (J) between the two side supports (L), as shown in *Figure 5*. Insert 1-1/4" screws through the center shelf (J) and into the edge of the back support (M), spacing them about 6" apart.

8. Repeat Steps 5 through 7 twice to construct two more shelf units.

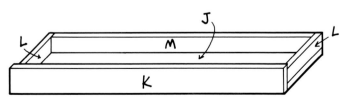

Figure 5

FINISHING

1. Fill any holes or crevices with wood filler.

2. Pre-fit the shutter doors in their openings, and plane or sand any surface that doesn't permit smooth opening of the doors. Then sand all surfaces of the cabinet, shutter doors, and center shelf units thoroughly.

3. Paint and/or stain each of the pieces the color of your choice. I chose an off-white to match the color of my wall.

4. Follow the manufacturer's instructions to attach the hinges to the painted shutter doors, spacing them exactly the same on all four doors. Then attach the hinges to the cabinet.

5. Attach a door pull to the front of each shutter door. Make certain that the pulls are positioned in exactly the same place on each door.

6. Attach the door latches to the inside of each of the four doors, following the manufacturer's instructions.

FINAL ASSEMBLY

1. The final assembly will probably require the assistance of a helper or two. Measure the length of the two cabinets and the shelves and mark their positions on the wall.

2. The cabinets are mounted by attaching wood strips to the wall and positioning the cabinets so that the undersides of their tops rest on the strips. Start by cutting one 32"-long wall support (N) from 1 x 3 pine. Position the wall support (N) on the wall, 3/4" lower than where the upper surface of the cabinet will be. Note that the wall support (N) is shorter than the cabinet top; this will allow you to shift the cabinet back and forth to center it over the support. Level the wall support (N) carefully and attach it to the wall using molly bolts or other secure methods.

3. Lift the cabinet and place it on top of the wall support (N) that is now attached to the wall. To secure the cabinet, drive four or five evenly spaced 3d finishing nails through its top (A) and into the wall

support (N). Recess the nail heads, carefully fill the nail holes, sand gently, and touch up the spot with paint or stain.

4. Position one shelf unit flush with the top of the mounted cabinet. Level it carefully and attach it to the adjoining cabinet side by inserting two 1-1/4" screws through the side support (L) and into the cabinet side (B). Attach the shelf to the wall using four evenly-spaced molly bolts, or other secure methods, bolting through the back support (M) into the wall.

5. Position the second shelf unit as desired and attach it to the cabinet and wall as before. Then attach the third shelf unit, making sure that it will be flush with the bottom of the adjoining cabinet.

6. Position the remaining cabinet on the opposite end of the shelf units. Repeat Steps 2 and 3 to attach the cabinet to the wall, and then attach the shelf units to the cabinet side (B) by following the procedure outlined in Step 4.

DESK ORGANIZER

It's always the small things in life that drive me right over the edge—like hunting for a pencil and paper to write down an address or telephone number. After fumbling through every desk drawer, I used to record important information with a magenta crayon stub on the back of my water bill, but all that has changed since I made this desk organizer. It has three drawers for note pads, pens, and pencils, and a shelf large enough to hold my phone.

SPECIAL TOOLS AND TECHNIQUES

Router and roundover bit (optional)

Mitering

MATERIALS AND SUPPLIES

8 linear feet of 1 x 4 pine

4 linear feet of 1 x 8 pine

6 linear feet of 1 x 10 pine

1 piece of 1/4"-thick plywood, 14" x 16"

HARDWARE

Approximately 50 #6 x 1-1/4" flathead wood screws

Approximately 50 3d finishing nails

1 small box of wire brads

3 decorative drawer pulls

CUTTING LIST

Code	Description	Qty.	Material	Dimensions
A	Top/Bottom	2	1 x 10 pine	26-1/4" long
B	Inner Divider	2	1 x 10 pine	3-5/8" long
C	Side	2	1 x 8 pine	9-1/4" long
D	Back	1	1 x 8 pine	27-3/4" long
E	Drawer Front/Back	6	1 x 4 pine	8" long
F	Drawer Side	6	1 x 4 pine	7-1/2" long
G	Drawer Bottom	3	1/4" plywood	6-3/4" x 7-3/4"

NOTES ON MATERIALS

Before you shop for the necessary materials for this project, check your workshop for scrap pieces and compare what you find with the pieces in the "Cutting List." Most of the wood you need may be lying around on your workshop floor!

MAKING THE FRAME

1. Cut two 26-1/4"-long top/bottom pieces (A) from 1 x 10 pine.

2. Cut two 3-5/8"-long inner dividers (B) from 1 x 10 pine.

3. Place the top/bottom pieces (A) on a level surface, parallel to each other, on edge, and 3-5/8" apart. Fit the two inner dividers (B) between the two top/bottom pieces (A), spacing them 8-1/4" from each other and from the ends, as shown in *Figure 1*. Glue the inner dividers (B) in place and drive three evenly spaced 1-1/4" screws through the top/bottom pieces (A) and into the edges of the inner dividers (B) at each joint.

4. From 1 x 8 pine, cut two 9-1/4"-long sides (C).

5. Position the sides (C) on the assembly as shown in *Figure 2*. Note that the sides (C) are flush at the front, back, and bottom of the assembly, but extend above the top face. Glue the sides (C) onto the ends of both of the top/bottom pieces (A) and

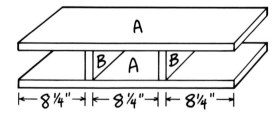

Figure 1

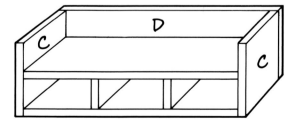

Figure 2

secure them in place with three 1-1/4" screws at each joint.

6. Cut one 27-3/4"-long back (D) from 1 x 8 pine.

7. Attach the back (D) to the assembly, as shown in *Figure 2*. Note that the back (D) is flush with the assembly at the bottom and at the sides, but extends above the top/bottom piece (A). Glue the back (D) to the edges of the top/bottom pieces (A) and to the ends of both sides (C). Drive three 1-1/4" screws through the back (D) at each joint.

8. If you own a router and roundover bit, use them to round the upper edges of the sides (C) and back (D). If you don't own a router, simply sand the edges with very rough sandpaper and then finish with increasingly fine grades of sandpaper.

MAKING THE DRAWERS

1. The three identical drawers for this organizer are constructed as shown in *Figure 3*. From 1 x 4 pine, cut six 8"-long drawer front/back pieces (E) and six 7-1/2"-long drawer sides (F).

2. To accommodate the plywood drawer bottoms (G), cut a 1/4" x 1/4" dado on the inside of every drawer piece (E and F), 3/8" from its lower edge.

3. Cut three 6-3/4" x 7-3/4" drawer bottoms (G) from 1/4"-thick plywood.

4. Assemble one drawer as shown in *Figure 3*. Note that the drawer front/back pieces (E) overlap the ends of the drawer sides (F). Use glue and 3d finishing nails at each end of the overlapping boards.

5. Repeat Step 4 two more times to assemble the remaining two drawers.

ADDING THE DRAWER TRIM

1. Each of the drawer fronts (E) is trimmed with 3/4"-wide decorative molding. To trim the first drawer front, cut and fit pieces of molding, mitering the ends so that they fit perfectly flush with the outer edges of the drawer front (E), as shown in *Figure 4*.

2. Glue the molding in place and use a tack hammer to drive tiny wire brads through the molding and into the drawer front (E). Recess the nails with a nail set.

3. Repeat Steps 1 and 2 twice more to trim the fronts of the remaining drawers with molding.

FINISHING

1. Fill any holes or crevices with wood filler.

2. Sand all surfaces of the completed drawers and frame thoroughly.

3. Paint or stain the completed desk organizer the colors of your choice. I chose pale green and mauve to match the colors in the room where my organizer makes its home.

4. Follow the manufacturer's instructions to install a drawer pull in the center of each drawer front.

5. Insert the drawers into the frame and begin organizing!

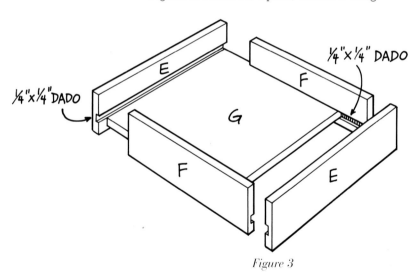

Figure 3

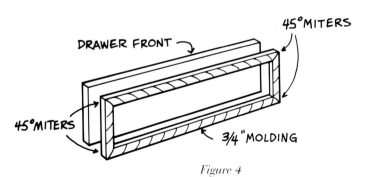

Figure 4

MULTIPLE PLANTER

If you're looking for a really attractive way to screen a portion of your window or deck, turn to page 69. You can't beat this multiple planter. It holds eight pots filled with your favorite sun-loving plants on its top, as well as shade-loving plants—or your favorite knickknacks—on the shelf beneath.

SPECIAL TECHNIQUES

Ripping

MATERIALS AND SUPPLIES

19 linear feet of 1 x 3 pine

70 linear feet of 1 x 4 pine

10 linear feet of 1 x 6 pine

12 linear feet of 1 x 10 pine

8 clay pots, 8" in diameter

HARDWARE

Approximately 100 #6 x 1-1/4" flathead wood screws

Approximately 250 #6 x 1-1/2" flathead wood screws

CUTTING LIST

Code	Description	Qty.	Material	Dimensions
A	Long Inner Frame	2	1 x 4 pine	70" long
B	Short Inner Frame	16	1 x 4 pine	7-1/4" long
C	Leg	14	1 x 4 pine	31" long
D	Leg Spacer	8	1 x 6 pine	13-1/8" long
E	Short Spacer	2	1 x 6 pine	3-1/4" long
F	Shelf	2	1 x 10 pine, ripped	70" long
G	Shelf Spacer	8	1 x 4 pine	13-1/8" long
H	Short Shelf Spacer	2	1 x 4 pine	3-1/4" long
I	Long Trim	2	1 x 3 pine	75" long
J	Short Trim	2	1 x 3 pine	7-1/4" long
K	Inner Trim	7	1 x 3 pine, ripped	7-1/4" long

NOTES ON MATERIALS

Check the diameters of the pots that you intend to place in the 7-1/4"-square planter openings. You can alter the planter dimensions if you wish, but you may find that it's easier to buy pots the right size. As you can see in the photo on page 69, the wider lips of the pots rest on the shelf spacers, while the narrower portions fit into the openings between the spacers.

If you plan to use your planter outdoors, buy galvanized screws and weather-resistant lumber and finish the completed project with outdoor paint or stain.

MAKING THE INNER FRAME

1. Cut two long inner frames (A) from 1 x 4 pine; each should be 70" long.

2. Cut 16 short inner frames (B) from 1 x 4 pine; each should be 7-1/4" long.

3. Glue two short inner frames (B) together to form a double thickness, as shown in *Figure 1*, and secure them by inserting four 1-1/4" screws, one near each corner.

4. Repeat Step 3 six more times to create a total of seven double-thick short inner frames (B). You'll have two single short inner frames (B) left over.

5. Place the two long inner frames (A) on edge, parallel to each other and 7-1/4" apart. Fit the double and single short inner frames (B) between the two long inner

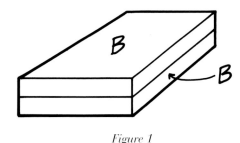

Figure 1

frames (A), as shown in *Figure 2*. Note that the single short inner frames (B) are on the ends of the assembly and that each of the openings measures 7-1/4" square. Glue the long inner frames (A) to the short inner frames (B) and insert two 1-1/2" screws through the long inner frames (A) and into the ends of the short inner frames (B) at each joint.

ADDING THE LEGS

1. Cut fourteen 31"-long legs (C) from 1 x 4 pine.

2. Cut eight leg spacers (D) from 1 x 6 pine, each measuring 13-1/8" long.

3. To attach five legs (C) and four leg spacers (D) to one side of the inner frame, first refer to *Figure 3*. Note that the top ends of the legs (C) and the upper edges of the leg spacers (D) should be flush with the top edges of the inner frame. Glue the legs (C) and spacers (D) in place and insert two 1-1/4" screws through each leg (C) and four 1-1/4" screws through each leg spacer (D) into the inner frame.

4. Turn the assembly over and repeat Step 3 to attach five legs (C) and four leg spacers (D) to the other side of the inner frame.

5. Cut two short spacers (E) from 1 x 6 pine, each measuring 3-1/4" long.

6. To attach two legs (C) and one short spacer (E) to one end of the inner frame, first refer to *Figure 4*. Note that the legs (C) to be attached will overlap the edges of the legs (C) already in place. Glue the two legs (C) and short spacer (E) in place and insert two 1-1/4" screws at each joint. Also insert 1-1/2" screws to join the overlapped legs (C) together, spacing the screws about 6" apart down the length of the legs (C) you've just added.

7. Repeat Step 6 to attach the remaining two legs (C) and short spacer (E) to the opposite end of the assembly.

ADDING THE SHELVES

1. Rip the 12 linear feet of 1 x 10 pine to a width of 8-3/4". Then cut two 70"-long shelves (F) from the ripped boards.

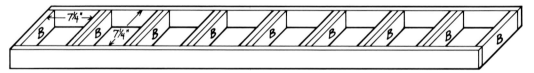

Figure 2

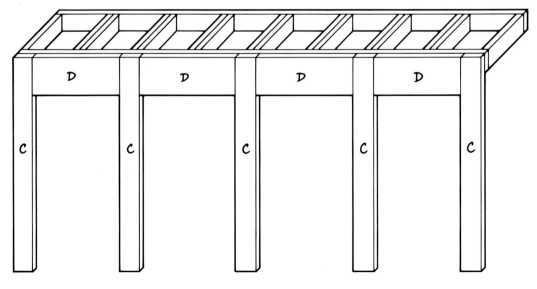

Figure 3

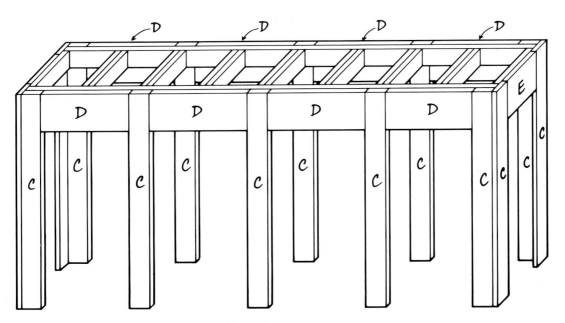

Figure 4

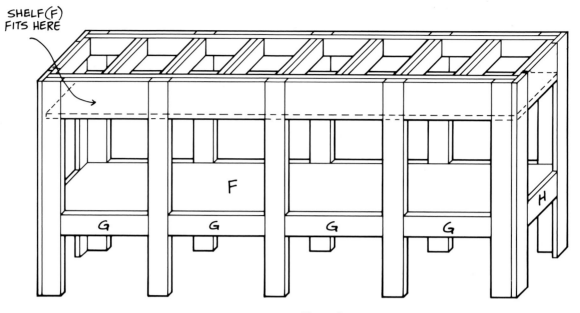

Figure 5

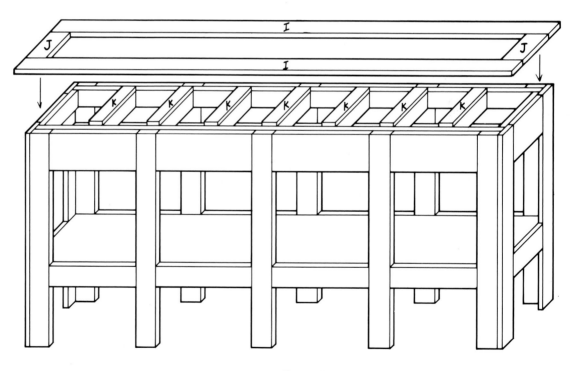

Figure 6

2. Glue the first shelf (F) in place inside the legs (C), positioning its bottom surface flush with the lower edges of the leg spacers (D) and short spacers (E), as shown in *Figure 5*. Secure the shelf in position by inserting two 1-1/2" screws through each leg (C), each leg spacer (D), and each short spacer (E) into the edges of the shelf (F).

3. Repeat Step 2 to attach the second shelf (F), positioning it 9-3/4" from the bottoms of the legs (C).

4. Cut eight shelf spacers (G) from 1 x 4 pine, each measuring 13-1/8".

5. Position four of the shelf spacers (G) between the legs on one side of the planter, as shown in *Figure 5*, placing their upper edges flush with the top face of the lower shelf (F). Glue the shelf spacers (G) in place and secure each one with two 1-1/2" screws driven through the spacer and into the edge of the shelf (F).

6. Repeat Step 5 to attach the remaining four shelf spacers (G) to the opposite side of the planter.

7. Cut two short shelf spacers (H) from 1 x 4 pine, each measuring 3-1/4" long.

8. Glue the short shelf spacers (H) in place between the legs (C) at both ends of the planter, positioning them so that their upper edges are flush with the top of the lower shelf (F). Secure each short shelf spacer (H) to the shelf (F) with two 1-1/2" screws.

ADDING THE TOP TRIM

1. Cut two long trim pieces (I) from 1 x 3 pine, each measuring 75" long.

2. Cut two short trim pieces (J) from 1 x 3 pine, each measuring 7-1/4" long.

3. Rip a 52" length of 1 x 3 to a width of 1-1/2".

4. Cut seven 7-1/4"-long inner trim pieces (K) from the 1-1/2"-wide ripped pine.

5. Glue the seven inner trim pieces (K) to the top edges of the seven double-thick short inner frames (B), as shown in *Figure 6*. Insert four 1-1/2" screws through each inner trim piece (K) and into the paired short inner frames (B) beneath.

6. Glue the two short trim pieces (J) and the two long trim pieces (I) to the top edges of the planter, so that their inner edges are flush with the inner faces of the long and short inner frames (A and B). Secure the trim pieces (J and I) with 1-1/2" screws spaced about 6" apart.

FINISHING

1. Fill all screw holes and crevices with wood filler.

2. Sand the entire planter thoroughly.

3. Paint or stain the completed planter the color of your choice.

Occasional Table

Everyone can use an extra table somewhere in the house, and because this occasional table is only 21" high and about 24" square, it will fit almost anywhere, too. If you have enough space, make a couple of these tables and place them side-by-side to create a good-looking coffee table.

Special Tools and Techniques

Bar clamps

Mitering

Materials and Supplies

18 linear feet of 1 x 4 pine

7 linear feet of 1 x 6 pine

1 piece of laminated pine, 17" x 17"

4 table legs, each 20" long

Hardware

Approximately 40 #6 x 1-1/4" flathead wood screws

Approximately 8 #10 x 3" flathead wood screws

Cutting List

Code	Description	Qty.	Material	Dimensions
A	Center Top	1	Laminated pine	17" x 17"
B	Top Trim	4	1 x 4 pine	24" long
C	Long Base	2	1 x 6 pine	24" long
D	Short Base	2	1 x 6 pine	13" long
E	Leg	4	Purchased	20" long
F	Rail	4	1 x 4 pine	Cut to fit (approx. 16-3/4" long)
G	Corner Support	4	1 x 4 pine	10" long

Notes on Materials

The center top (A) of this occasional table is made from laminated pine boards. Most building-supply stores sell sections of wood that have already been laminated. You can laminate the boards yourself, of course, but we don't recommend doing so unless you're an experienced woodworker and own the necessary tools. The monetary savings aren't that significant, and you'll save a lot of time by purchasing the laminated pine.

If you don't have a lathe or don't want to turn the legs yourself, just purchase four turned legs from a building-supply store. The shape of the legs isn't important, but the four faces at the top of each one must be flat in order to provide proper connections for the rails that abut them.

Constructing the Table Top

1. Cut one 17" x 17" center top (A) from laminated pine.

2. Cut four 24"-long top trim pieces (B) from 1 x 4 pine.

3. Set each top trim piece (B) on its face and miter each end of all four pieces at a 45-degree angle, as shown in *Figure 1*. When you're finished, one edge of each top trim piece should be 17" long and the opposite edge should be 24" long.

4. Glue and clamp the top trim pieces (B) to the edges of the table top (A) and leave the assembly undisturbed for at least 24 hours. The framed top should measure 24" x 24".

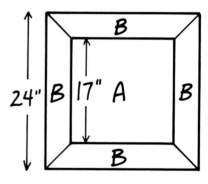

Figure 1

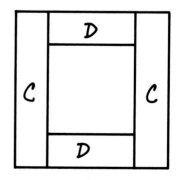

Figure 2

Constructing the Base Frame and Legs

1. Cut two long base pieces (C) from 1 x 6 pine, each 24" long.

2. Cut two short base pieces (D) from 1 x 6 pine, each 13" long.

3. To assemble the base frame, place the two long base pieces (C) on a level surface, parallel to each other and 13" apart.

Place the two short base pieces (D) between the long base pieces (C) to form a 24" x 24" square, as shown in *Figure 2*. Glue and clamp the four pieces together. Leave the assembly undisturbed for at least 24 hours.

4. To add the four 20"-long legs, you must first center each one in a corner of the base frame. To locate the center point for a leg, draw a line across a long base

piece (C) 5-1/2" from the end, as shown in *Figure 3*, to form a 5-1/2" x 5-1/2" square. Then draw two lines to connect each set of opposite corners in that square. The intersection of these two lines is the center point for the leg.

5. Most purchased legs come with a metal screw in the center of the top of the leg. At the marked center point on the long base (C), drill a hole slightly smaller in diameter than the metal screw. Apply glue to the meeting surfaces and hand-screw the leg (E) into the drilled hole. Make certain that the leg is positioned so that the flat faces at its top are parallel to the edges of the table.

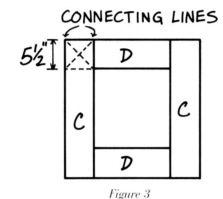

Figure 3

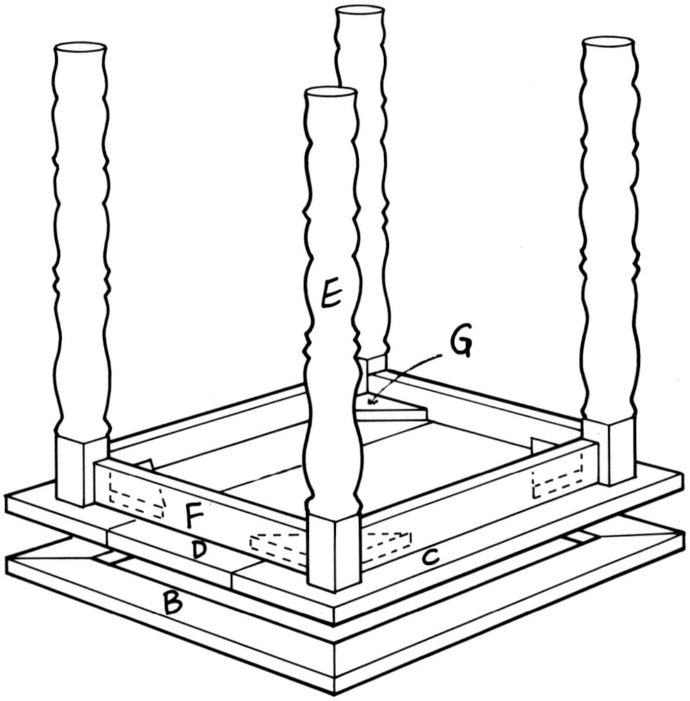

6. Repeat Step 5 to attach the remaining three legs (E) to the other three corners of the base frame.

7. Make certain that all four legs (E) are perfectly straight. Then let the assembly dry overnight until the glue sets.

8. To reinforce the leg joints, turn the base assembly right-side up. Insert two 3" screws through the each long base (C) and into each leg (E).

ADDING THE RAILS

1. Before cutting the four rails (F) from 1 x 3 pine, measure the distance between each set of table legs. This measurement will vary, depending upon the diameter of the legs you purchased. Then cut each rail piece (F) to that length.

2. Glue one rail (F) between each set of two adjacent legs (E), as shown in *Figure 4*. Then insert 1-1/4" screws, spaced 6" apart, through the long bases (C) and short bases (D) and into the edges of the rails (F).

3. Cut four 10"-long corner supports (G) from 1 x 4 pine. Set the corner supports on their faces and miter the ends of each one at 45-degree angles.

4. To further reinforce the rails (F) and legs (E), glue a corner support (G) between each set of two rails (F), as shown in *Figure 4*. Insert 1-1/4" screws through the corner support and into the base frame.

ADDING THE TABLE TOP

1. Place the center top (A) and attached trim pieces (B) upside down on a level surface.

2. Center the base assembly over the top assembly, so that the sides of the assemblies are exactly flush (see *Figure 4*). Glue the assemblies together and insert 1-1/4" screws, spaced 6" apart, through the long and short base pieces (C and D) into the top assembly.

FINISHING

1. Fill any cracks, crevices, or screw holes with wood filler. Then sand all surfaces of the occasional table thoroughly.

2. Paint or stain the completed project the color of your choice.

Figure 4

SUN LOUNGE WITH PLANTERS

The combination planter and sun lounge shown on page 77 makes an attractive addition to any patio, deck, or pool. A standard chaise-lounge cushion—available almost anywhere—fits the lounge easily, and the planters on both ends are large enough to hold a wealth of cheerful flowers or greenery.

SPECIAL TECHNIQUES

Mitering

MATERIALS AND SUPPLIES

52 linear feet of 1 x 3 pine

85 linear feet of 1 x 4 pine

1 sheet of 3/4"-thick plywood, 4' x 8'

HARDWARE

Approximately 500 #6 x 1-1/4" flathead wood screws

Approximately 30 #6 x 2-1/2" flathead wood screws

Approximately 60 3d finishing nails

Eight 3/8"-diameter bolts, at least 3" long, with matching wing nuts

CUTTING LIST

Code	Description	Qty.	Material	Dimensions
A	Side	34	1 x 4 pine	23" long
B	Long Support	4	1 x 3 pine	21" long
C	Medium Support	4	1 x 3 pine	10" long
D	Short Support	16	1 x 3 pine	6" long
E	Base	2	3/4" plywood	See *Fig. 2*
F	Bottom	2	3/4" plywood	See *Fig. 2*
G	Trim	12	1 x 3 pine	Cut to fit (approx. 128" total)
H	Long Frame	2	1 x 4 pine	72" long
I	Short Frame	2	1 x 4 pine	21" long
J	Long Lounge Support	2	1 x 3 pine	70-1/2" long
K	Short Lounge Support	6	1 x 3 pine	19-1/2" long
L	Lounge Platform	1	3/4" plywood	19-1/2" x 70-1/2"

NOTES ON MATERIALS

If the finished project will be exposed to the elements, choose materials, hardware, glue, and a wood finish that are suited for exterior use. We used pressure-treated pine to build our sun lounge, but redwood, western cedar, or other exterior-grade woods make good substitutes. Depending upon the type of wood you buy (each is likely to have a different finish cut), you may need to trim the plywood base and bottom of the planter to fit properly.

MAKING THE PLANTER SIDES

1. The six sides (one long, one medium, and four short) of each planter are different widths and contain different numbers of 1 x 4s. The long side has six 1 x 4s, the medium side has three, and the four short sides have two each. To start building the twelve sides for both planters, first cut thirty-four 23"-long sides (A) from 1 x 4 pine.

2. Cut four long supports (B) from 1 x 3 pine, each measuring 21" long.

3. Lay six of the side pieces (A) on a level surface, positioning them parallel to each other as shown in *Figure 1*. Adjust the

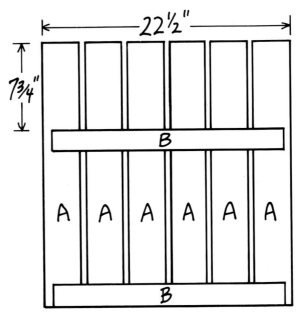

Figure 1

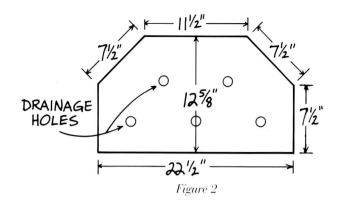

Figure 2

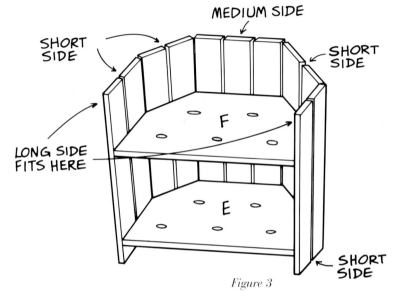

Figure 3

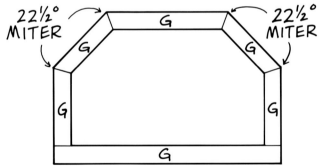

Figure 4

spacing between the side pieces (A) so that the total width is exactly 22-1/2". Glue one long support (B) flush with the ends of all six side pieces (A). Note that there is a 3/4" inset at each end of this long support (B). Secure the long support (B) to the side pieces (A) by inserting two 1-1/4" screws through the long support (B) and into each side piece (A).

4. Attach the remaining long support (B), 7-3/4" from the other ends of the six side pieces (A), as shown in *Figure 1* and described in Step 3.

5. Repeat Steps 3 and 4 to construct another long side for the second planter.

6. Cut four 10"-long medium supports (C) from 1 x 4 pine.

7. The medium sides, one for each planter, are constructed in the same manner as the long sides—but each one contains only three side pieces (A) and these are spaced differently. Lay three side pieces (A) parallel to each other on a level surface. Adjust the spacing between them so that the total width is exactly 11-1/2". Glue and attach the medium supports (C) as explained in Steps 3 and 4, leaving a 3/4" overlap at each end of each medium support (C).

8. Repeat Step 7 to make another medium side for the second planter.

9. Cut sixteen 6"-long short supports (D) from 1 x 4 pine.

10. Lay two side pieces (A) parallel to each other on a level surface. Adjust the spacing between the side pieces (A) so that the total width is exactly 7-1/2". Attach two short supports (D) to the two side pieces (A), following the instructions in Steps 3 and 4.

11. Repeat Step 10 seven more times to build all the short sides for both planters.

Adding the Bottoms and Bases

1. Using *Figure 2* as a guide, cut four identical pieces from 3/4"-thick exterior-grade plywood. Two pieces will be bases (E) and two will be bottoms (F) for the planters.

2. To allow for drainage, drill five 1"-diameter holes in each base (E) and bottom (F), as shown in *Figure 2*. The exact placement of these holes is not important.

3. To attach each base (E) to each side assembly, first position the base over the lower supports (B, C, and D), as shown in *Figure 3*. If necessary, trim the base to fit. Glue the base (E) in place and insert 1-1/4" screws through it and into the edges of the supports (B, C, and D), using two screws at each joint. Also insert two 1-1/4" screws through each of the side pieces (A) and into the edges of each base (E).

4. Fit a planter bottom (F) into each assembly, as shown in *Figure 3*, making certain that the bottom rests evenly on its supports (B, C, and D) and is level inside the assembly. Glue the bottom (F) in place and insert two 1-1/4" screws through it and into each of the supports (B, C, and D). Also insert two screws through each of the side pieces (A) and into the edges of each bottom.

COMPLETING THE PLANTER

1. Measure carefully and cut lengths of trim (G) from 1 x 3 pine to cover the exposed top edges of the planters, as shown in *Figure 4*. Note that some of the trim pieces (G) must be mitered at a 22-1/2-degree angle on one or both ends.

2. Glue the trim pieces (G) to the exposed upper ends of the planter side pieces (A). Secure the trim in place with 3d finishing nails spaced about 2" apart.

CONSTRUCTING THE SUN LOUNGE FRAME

1. Cut two long frames (H) from 1 x 4 pine, each 72" long.

2. Cut two short frames (I) from 1 x 4 pine, each 21" long.

3. Place the two long frames (H) on a level surface, parallel to each other, on edge,

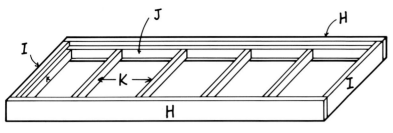

Figure 5

and 21" apart. Glue the two short frames (I) between the ends of the long frames, as shown in *Figure 5*. Then insert 1-1/4" screws through the long frames (H) and into the ends of the short frames (I), using two screws at each joint.

4. Cut two long lounge supports (J), each 70-1/2", from 1 x 3 pine.

5. Glue each long lounge support (J) to the inside of each long frame (H), 3/4" from the top edge of the long frame. Secure the parts by inserting 1-1/4" screws spaced 6" apart.

6. Cut six short lounge supports (K), each 19-1/2" long, from 1 x 3 pine.

7. Glue one short lounge support (K) to the inside of each short frame (I), 3/4" from the top edge of the short frame. Use 1-1/4" screws spaced 6" apart to secure the two short lounge supports in place.

8. Glue the remaining four short lounge supports (K) between the two long lounge supports (J), spacing them approximately 13" apart. Insert two 2-1/2" screws through the long frames (H) and the long lounge supports (J) into each end of each short lounge support (K).

9. Cut one 19-1/2" x 70-1/2" lounge platform (L) from 3/4"-thick plywood.

10. Glue the lounge platform (L) to the top edges of the lounge supports (J and K). Insert 1-1/4" screws, spacing them 6" apart, through the lounge platform and into the lounge supports.

FINAL ASSEMBLY AND FINISHING

1. The two planters must now be connected to the lounge. In order to determine the correct placement, first take a look at the project photo. Note that we attached our lounge so that the cushion would rise slightly above the planters. Place your cushion on top of the lounge and measure the distance from the bottom of the lounge frame to the top of the cushion. Using this measurement as a guide, mark across the long side of each planter to indicate where you'd like to locate the bottom of the lounge. Make sure that the mark you've just made is no more than 9" down from the upper face of the planter trim, or the bolts you insert to attach the lounge to the planters will end up being below the base (F), and you won't be able to reach them in order to tighten the wing nuts onto them.

2. Drill four equally-spaced holes, slightly larger in diameter than the bolts, through each short lounge support (K) and the short frame (I) to which it's attached.

3. Enlist the services of a helper and, holding the lounge at the marked location on each planter, mark the corresponding hole locations on one long side of each planter. Then drill bolt holes in the planter side at the marked locations.

4. Fit the 3/8" bolts through the drilled holes in the lounge and through the long side of each planter. Add the wing nuts, tightening the nuts firmly to connect the lounge securely.

5. You may have noticed that the lounge in the photo has additional lounge supports underneath it. These really aren't necessary. We added them because we have groups of very large teenage boys involved in horseplay around our pool. If you'd like to add the supports, just attach a length of 1 x 2 to each planter side, 3/4" below the lower edges of the lounge. Then slip two or three 70" lengths of 1 x 4 between these supports and the bottom of the lounge.

6. Sand the completed project thoroughly.

7. Stain or paint the sun lounge and planters the color of your choice.

TILED KITCHEN TABLE

If your kitchen is small, the table shown on the next page may be the answer to the problem of limited space. Although its top measures only 29" x 46", the table is large enough to hold a hearty breakfast for two and can also serve as an additional work surface. Select tile colors—and paint colors if you choose to paint the table—to match your kitchen decor.

SPECIAL TOOLS AND TECHNIQUES

3 or 4 bar clamps

Saber saw or large chisel

Trowel for spreading mastic

Rubber-surfaced trowel for applying grout

Tile cutter (if necessary)

Mitering

MATERIALS AND SUPPLIES

9-1/2 linear feet of 1 x 3 pine

12 linear feet of 1 x 4 pine

22 linear feet of 1 x 6 pine

2 linear feet of 2 x 6 pine

1 piece of 1/2"-thick plywood, 22" x 40"

9-1/2 linear feet of 2-1/2"-wide baseboard molding

4 decorative table legs, each 3-1/2" x 3-1/2" at the top

40 tiles, each 4" x 4" (or enough tiles of a different size to cover an area 21-3/4" x 39")

Small containers of tile grout, mastic, and sealer

HARDWARE

Approximately 50 #6 x 1-1/4" flathead wood screws

Approximately 50 #6 x 2" flathead wood screws

Approximately 30 #10 x 3" flathead wood screws

Approximately 50 3d finishing nails

CUTTING LIST

Code	Description	Qty.	Material	Dimensions
A	Long Top Frame	2	1 x 4 pine	46" long
B	Short Top Frame	2	1 x 4 pine	21-3/4" long
C	Center Top	1	1/2" plywood	21-3/4" x 39"
D	Table Leg	4	3-1/2" x 3-1/2" newel post	27" long
E	Long Side Rail	2	1 x 6 pine	38" long
F	Short Side Rail	2	1 x 6 pine	20-3/4" long
G	Corner Support	4	2 x 6 pine	5-1/2" on short sides
H	Short Bottom Frame	2	1 x 6 pine	28-3/4" long
I	Long Bottom Frame	2	1 x 6 pine	35" long
J	Long Trim	2	1 x 3 pine	34-1/2" long
K	Short Trim	2	1 x 3 pine	17-1/4" long
L	Long Molding	2	2-1/2"-wide molding	34-1/2" long
M	Short Molding	2	2-1/2"-wide molding	17-1/4" long

NOTES ON MATERIALS

If you don't own a lathe or don't want to turn the table legs yourself, simply follow our lead by purchasing four newel posts from a building-supply store and cutting them to length. When they're turned upside down, the posts make extremely attractive table legs—and who would guess?

Be sure to purchase exterior-grade plywood for the center top (C). Also buy a few extra tiles; they're breakable, and "stuff happens."

Most tiles sold at building-supply stores are now "self-spacing"; they come with small projections on their edges so that when you lay the tiles out, the grout lines between them will be even. Because the spacing is determined by individual tile manufacturers and because the actual size of a so-called 4" tile can vary slightly from manufacturer to manufacture, we recommend that you check your tile design. Slight variations in tile size and spacing can increase or decrease the finished table-top dimensions significantly, so before you cut any wood, make certain that your tiles will fit the dimensions we've provided. Here's how:

Arrange your tiles on the uncut piece of 1/2"-thick plywood. We arranged five rows of nine tiles each,

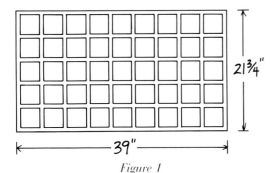

Figure 1

as shown in *Figure 1*. Draw a rectangle around the length and width of your tile arrangement, allowing for a border of grout around the outer edges that is the same width as the grout between the tiles. Then measure the rectangle. Compare the dimensions of this rectangle to the size specified in the instructions for the center top (C)—21-3/4" x 39". If your measurements deviate from these, adjust the size of the center top (C) and the lengths of the other table-top pieces (A, B, H, and I)—or cut your tiles to fit.

To ensure that the finished table top will be flat, check to see that the thickness of the plywood plus the combined thickness of the tiles you plan to use and the mastic you place under it will equal the thickness of the 1 x 4 pine pieces (A and B) that will border the table top (see *Figure 2*). You can alter the thickness of the mastic underneath the tiles by a very small amount, but to make significant alternations, you'll need to alter the thickness of either the plywood or the tile.

CONSTRUCTING THE TABLE TOP

1. The table top is composed of a top and bottom layer. The top layer consists of two long top frames (A) and two short top frames (B), which surround the center top (C), as shown in *Figure 2*. The bottom layer will be attached to the table base later. To make the top layer, start by cutting two 46" lengths of 1 x 4 pine and labeling each one as a long top frame (A). Cut two 21-3/4" lengths of 1 x 4 pine and label them as short top frames (B).

2. Cut a 21-3/4" x 39" piece of 1/2"-thick plywood and label it as the center top (C).

3. Place the center top (C) on a level surface. Position the short and long top frames (A and B) along the outer edges of the center top (C), as shown in *Figure 2*. Glue the frame pieces (A and B) to the center top (C), checking to make certain that the assembly is perfectly square.

Clamp the five pieces of wood together with bar clamps for at least 24 hours.

CONSTRUCTING THE TABLE BASE

1. The newel posts will serve as the table legs (D). Cut each one to 27" in length, being careful to not to cut off the decorative ends.

2. In order to support the long and short side rails (E and F) of the kitchen table, you must remove a 1-3/4" x 1-3/4" x 5-1/2" corner section from the inside of the square top of each leg. Set the depth of your saber saw to 1-3/4" and make three cuts in the order shown in *Figure 3*. (The blade edges in the illustration indicate the direction in which these cuts should be made.) These cuts may be made with a chisel rather than a saber saw.

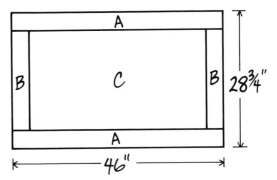

Figure 2

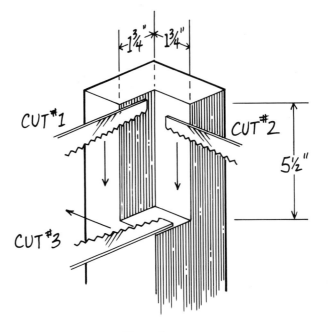

Figure 3

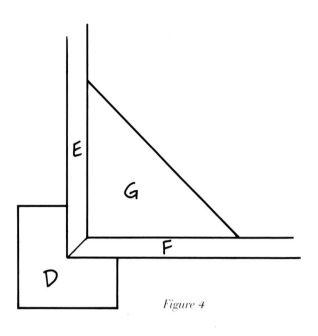

Figure 4

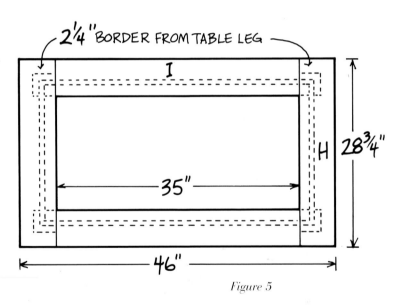

2¼" BORDER FROM TABLE LEG

Figure 5

3. Take a good look at *Figure 4*. The long and short side rails (E and F) that connect the table legs (D) are cut from 1 x 6 pine. Cut two 38"-long boards from 1 x 6 pine and label them as long side rails (E). Cut two 20-3/4"-long boards from 1 x 6 pine and label them as short side rails (F). Set each of the four pieces (E and F) on edge and miter each end of each board at a 45-degree angle, as shown in *Figure 4*.

4. This step probably requires the assistance of a willing helper (or an unwilling helper and substantial financial remuneration) and should be performed on a level surface. Each of the legs (D) must be connected to the long and short side rails (E and F), and the entire assembly must be perfectly level. This is easiest to accomplish if you work with the legs upside down. (For help in making sure your project is level, see page 11.)

Carefully fit the end of one long side rail (E) and one short side rail (F) inside the opening that you previously cut in one leg (D), matching the miters as you do (see *Figure 4*). Glue the rails to the leg and to each other, then insert two 2" screws through each of the rails (E and F) and into the leg. Repeat the process to attach the remaining three legs (D) to the remaining two side rails (E and F). A word of caution: It's easy to get so involved in what you're doing that you forget you're constructing a rectangular base. Don't forget that the two short side rails (F) must be opposite each other on the base; the two long side rails (E) must also be opposite each other.

5. Cut four triangular corner supports (G) from 2 x 6 pine. These should measure 5-1/2" on each of their two short sides. To attach one in each of the four corners, as shown in *Figure 6*, glue them flush with the top of the legs and rails. Then insert two 3" screws through each corner support (G) and into each set of side rails (E and F).

ADDING THE BOTTOM LAYER OF THE TABLE TOP

1. The bottom layer of the table top, which consists of four lengths of 1 x 6 pine, adds visual thickness and also supports the center plywood. In order to avoid creating screw holes in the table top, the bottom layer is connected first to the table base assembly. Start by cutting two 28-3/4" lengths from 1 x 6 pine and labeling them as short bottom frames (H). Also cut two 35" lengths from 1 x 6 pine and label them as long bottom frames (I).

2. Place the short bottom frames (H) and long bottom frames (I) on a flat surface, positioning the long bottom frames (I) inside the short bottom frames (H), as shown in *Figure 5*. The resulting rectangle should measure 28-3/4" x 46".

3. Turn the assembled table base upside down and center it over the four bottom pieces (H and I). You should have a 2-1/4"-wide border outside each of the four table legs (D). This dimension may vary slightly if you've altered the dimensions of your table top.

4. Apply glue to the upper edges of the long and short side rails (E and F), the exposed ends of the table legs (D), and the upper faces of the corner supports (G). To hold the assembly together, insert 2" screws diagonally through the inner faces of the long and short side rails (E and F) and into the bottom frame pieces (H and I), spacing the screws about 6" apart.

5. Turn the assembly right side up. To further stabilize the table, insert two 3" screws through the bottom frame pieces (H and I) and into each table leg (D). Also insert 1-1/4" screws through the bottom frame pieces (H and I) and into the upper edges of the long and short side rails (E and F).

JOINING THE TABLE TOP TO THE BASE

1. Turn the top assembly (pieces A, B, and C) upside down on a flat surface. Make certain that the side which will accommodate the tiles is face down. Place the base assembly upside-down over the top

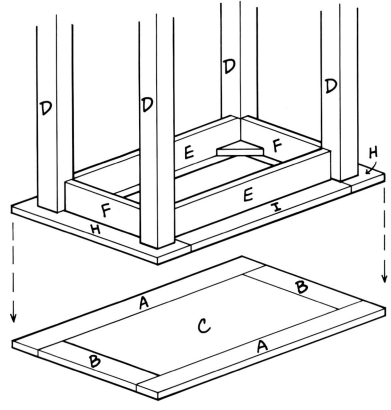

Figure 6

assembly, as shown in *Figure 6*. The two short bottom frame pieces (H) and the two long bottom frame pieces (I) should be flush with the outer edges of the top assembly. The inner edges of the bottom frame pieces (H and I) will overlap the center top (C) by 2".

2. Glue the four bottom frame pieces (H and I) to the top assembly. Then drive four 1-1/4" screws through each short bottom frame piece (H) and five 1-1/4" screws through each long bottom piece (I) into the long and short top frames (A and B). Space the screws evenly along the length of each board. Allow the glue to dry and then turn the assembled table right side up.

ADDING THE TRIM

1. Next, you'll add the trim to the outside faces of the side rails (E and F). We added a length of 1 x 3 pine just under the table top and a length of 2-1/2"-wide baseboard molding below that. Although our measurements should be very close to the cutting size for the trim, we suggest that you measure between your table legs before cutting the trim pieces, since your assembly may vary slightly. Even a 1/32" error on a trim piece will make your project look less than professional.

Cut two long trim pieces (J) from 1 x 3 pine, each measuring 34-1/2" in length. Cut two short trim pieces (K) from 1 x 3 pine, each measuring 17-1/4" in length.

2. Glue the first long trim piece (J) onto one long side rail (E) between the table legs (D). The upper edge of the long trim (J) should be flush against the bottom of the table top. Insert 3d finishing nails to attach the long trim piece (J) in place, spacing the nails about 6" apart and countersinking each one. Repeat to attach the remaining long trim piece (J) to the opposite side of the table.

3. Glue the first short trim piece (K) onto one short side rail (F) between the table legs (D), with its top edge flush against the bottom of the table top. Insert 3d finishing nails to attach the short trim piece (K) in place, spacing the nails about 6" apart and countersinking each one. Repeat to attach the remaining short trim piece (K) to the opposite side of the table.

4. Cut two 34-1/2"-long pieces of 2-1/2"-wide baseboard molding (L). Cut two 17-1/4"-long pieces of 2-1/2"-wide baseboard molding (M).

5. Glue the two long molding pieces (L) beneath the long trim pieces (J) and between the two table legs (D) and secure with 3d finishing nails spaced about 6" apart. Countersink these nails as before.

6. Glue the two short molding pieces (M) beneath the short trim pieces (K) in the same way that you attached the long molding pieces (L) in Step 5.

ADDING THE TILE

1. Following the manufacturer's directions carefully and using a mastic trowel, spread an even coat of tile mastic over the surface of the plywood center top (C).

2. Place the tiles on the mastic one at a time, making sure that they are absolutely straight. Do not slide them, or the mastic will be forced up onto the sides of the tiles. Let the mastic dry overnight.

3. Mix the tile grout according the manufacturer's directions (or use pre-mixed grout).

4. Using a rubber-surfaced grout trowel, spread the grout over the tiles with arcing motions. Hold the trowel at an angle so that the grout is forced evenly into the spaces between the tiles.

5. When the grout begins to set up, use a damp rag to wipe the excess from the tiles and joints. If you let the grout harden too long, it will be very difficult to remove. Use as little water as possible when removing the excess so that you don't thin the grout that remains. Let the grout dry overnight.

6. Use a damp rag to wipe the remaining film from the tile.

7. Apply grout sealer, following the manufacturer's directions, which may tell you to wait several days before applying the sealer to the project.

FINISHING

1. Fill any screw holes with wood filler.

2. Thoroughly sand all wood portions of the completed table.

3. Stain or paint the wood portions of the table the color of your choice.

DESK/CABINET

My son needed a desk for studying, but finding enough space in his room amongst the golf clubs, baseball cards, girlfriend's pictures, painting easel, and basketball hoops was difficult. To solve this problem, we came up with a project that provides a large surface when the desktop is extended (see page 87) but that saves space when it's closed (see page 91).

SPECIAL TOOLS

Two pipe clamps

Router: Although it's possible, making this project without a router is difficult and time-consuming. If you don't own a router, we suggest that you borrow one from a friend.

MATERIALS AND SUPPLIES

3 linear feet of 3/4" x 3/4" pine

9 linear feet of 1 x 3 pine

16 linear feet of 1 x 4 pine

9 linear feet of 1 x 12 pine

3/8"-diameter dowel rod, at least 2" long

3 pieces of laminated pine, each measuring 30" x 36"

1 piece of 3/4"-thick plywood, 30" x 40"

NOTES ON MATERIALS

The sides, cabinet doors, and desktop are constructed of laminated 1 x 4 pine boards. Most building-supply stores sell sections of pine that have already been laminated. You can laminate the boards yourself, of course, but I don't recommend doing so unless you're an experienced woodworker and have the necessary tools.

HARDWARE

Approximately 200 #6 x 1-1/4" flathead wood screws

Approximately 10 3d finishing nails

Two round cabinet knobs for the front of the cabinet.

2 rectangular cabinet pulls with recessed and hinged handles

2 concealed cabinet hinges

CUTTING LIST

Code	Description	Qty.	Material	Dimensions
A	Desktop	1	Laminated pine	23-1/2" x 35-3/4"
B	Desktop Brace	2	1 x 3 pine	6" long
C	Dowel Rod	2	3/8" dowel rod	1" long
D	Desktop Front	1	1 x 4 pine	35-3/4" long
E	Desktop Support	2	1 x 4 pine	2-3/4" long
F	Desktop Inner Support	1	3/4" x 3/4" pine	34-1/4" long
G	Side	2	Laminated pine	15" x 29-1/2"
H	Back	1	3/4" plywood	29-1/2" x 37-1/2"
I	Inner Support	6	1 x 3 pine	9-3/4" long
J	Shelf	2	1 x 12 pine	36" long
K	Top	1	1 x 12 pine	36" long
L	Top Support	1	1 x 4 pine	34" long
M	Trim	3	1 x 4 pine	36" long
N	Bottom Trim	1	1 x 3 pine	36" long
O	Cabinet Door	2	Laminated pine	17-3/4" x 25-1/4"

MAKING THE DESKTOP

1. Cut one 23-1/2" x 35-3/4" desktop (A) from laminated pine.

2. Cut two 6"-long desktop braces (B) from 1 x 3 pine.

3. Attach one desktop brace (B) to the desktop (A), as shown in *Figure 1*, using glue and two 1-1/4" screws. Note that the ends of the desktop brace (B) and the desktop (A) are flush and that the 6"-long

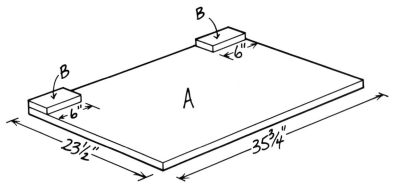

Figure 1

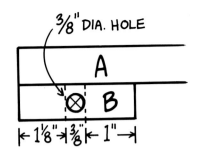

3/8" DIA. HOLE

A

⊗ B

← 1⅛" →← ⅜" →← 1" →

Figure 2

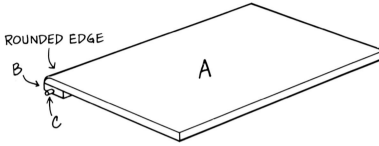

ROUNDED EDGE

B

A

C

Figure 3

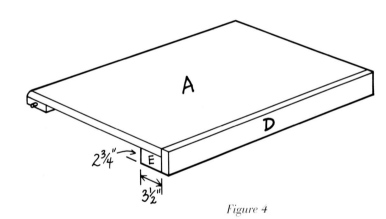

A

D

2¾" → E

3½"

Figure 4

edge of the desktop brace (B) is flush with the 35-3/4"-long edge of the desktop (A).

4. Repeat Step 3 to attach the remaining desktop brace (B) to the opposite end of the desktop (A).

5. Each of the desktop braces (B) must now be drilled to accept a dowel rod (C). Using the placement dimensions given in *Figure 2*, drill a 3/8"-diameter hole, 1/2" deep, in the end of one desktop brace (B).

6. Repeat Step 5 to drill a 3/8"-diameter hole, 1/2" deep, in the end of the other desktop brace (B). The second hole must be drilled as a mirror-image of the first hole.

7. Using a router and roundover bit, round the 35-3/4"-long edge of the desktop (A) to which the desktop braces (B) are attached, as shown in *Figure 3*.

8. Cut two 1"-long pieces of 3/8"-diameter dowel rod (C).

9. Apple glue to one end of each dowel rod (C) and insert the rods into the holes drilled in the desktop brace (B). Each rod should protrude 1/2" from its hole.

10. Cut one 35-3/4"-long desktop front (D) from 1 x 4 pine.

11. Glue the desktop front (D) to the unrouted 35-3/4"-long edge of the desktop (A), as shown in *Figure 4*. Secure the desktop front (D) by driving 1-1/4" screws, spaced about 6" apart, through its face and into the edge of the desktop (A).

12. Cut two 2-3/4"-long desktop supports (E) from 1 x 4 pine.

13. Glue one desktop support (E) flush with the ends of the desktop front (D) and the desktop (A), as shown in *Figure 4*. Drive two 1-1/4" screws through the face of the desktop (A) into the edge of the desktop support (E) and two more screws through the face of the desktop front (D) into the end of the desktop support (E).

14. Repeat Step 13 to attach the remaining desktop support (E) to the opposite ends of the desktop front (D) and the desktop (A).

15. Cut one 34-1/4"-long desktop inner support (F) from 3/4" x 3/4" pine.

16. Glue and nail the desktop inner support (F) between the two desktop supports (E), over the joint formed by the desktop (A) and the desktop front (D). Secure the support (F) to both the desktop (A) and desktop front (D) by inserting 1-1/4" nails, spaced about 4" apart, along its length.

CONSTRUCTING THE OUTER CABINET

1. Cut two 15" x 29-1/2" sides (G) from laminated pine.

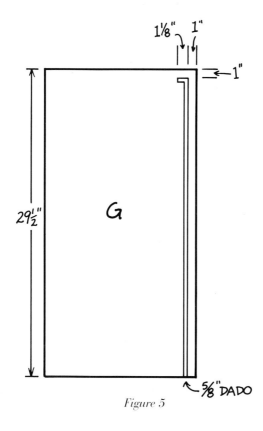

1⅛" 1"

←1"

29½"

G

⤹ 5/8" DADO

Figure 5

2. A dado must be cut in each of the two sides (G) to accommodate the dowel rods (C) in the desktop assembly. Using *Figure 5* as a placement guide, cut a 5/8"-wide dado, 1/2" deep, 1" from one 29-1/2" edge of one side (G). Note that the dado stops 1" from the upper end of the side (G), turns 90 degrees, and proceeds 1-1/8" further.

3. Repeat Step 2 to dado the remaining side (G), keeping in mind that the two dadoed sides (G) must be mirror images of each other when you're finished.

4. Cut one 37-1/2" x 29-1/2" back (H) from 3/4"-thick plywood.

5. At this point, you should perform what's known as a "dry assembly"—a temporary assembly using screws but no glue—to make certain that the desktop assembly will fit and slide easily inside the dadoes cut into the two sides (G). This particular step will be easier if you can find a willing helper to assist.

First, using only as many screws as needed to hold the parts together, attach the back (H) over the edges of the two sides (G), as shown in *Figure 6*, with the mirror-image dadoes in the sides (G) placed at the back of the assembly. Insert the screws through the back (H) and into the edges of the sides (G). Now turn the assembly upside down.

6. To hold the open front edges of the sides (G) exactly 36" apart, attach two pipe clamps to them.

7. Now you need to test-fit the desktop assembly by slipping the dowel rods (C) protruding from its ends into the dadoes in the sides (G) of the cabinet. To do this, hold the desktop assembly vertically over the partly assembled cabinet, with the top face of the desktop (A) facing the inner surface of the cabinet back (H) and the desktop front (D) facing down. Fit the dowel rods (C) into the dadoes in the two sides (G), and gently lower the desktop assembly into the cabinet.

8. Carefully turn the entire assembly right side up. Pull the desktop front (D) upward and forward towards the open front of the cabinet, making certain that the dowel

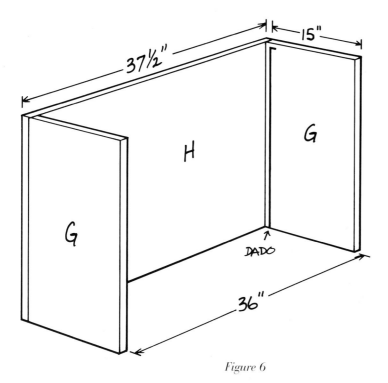

15"

37½"

H

G

G

DADO

36"

Figure 6

rods (C) glide easily within the dadoes, and that the desktop assembly will rotate from a vertical to a horizontal position when you reach the top of the dadoes. If the movement isn't smooth, now is the time to correct it. You may have to enlarge the dadoes at places where the dowel rods (C) bind, sand down the rods slightly, or further round the back edge of the desktop assembly.

9. When the assembly works to your satisfaction, disassemble the structure, set the desktop assembly aside, and reassemble the back (H) and two sides (G), this time using glue and inserting 1-1/4" screws about 6" apart along the length of each joint.

10. Cut six 9-3/4"-long inner supports (I) from 1 x 3 pine.

11. Using *Figure 7* as a placement guide, glue three of the inner supports (I) to one side (G). Position the first inner support (I) 1-1/2" from the upper end of the side (G); the second inner support (I) 14-1/2" from the same end; and the third inner support (I) 1/4" from the bottom end. Note that all three supports (I) should be 1-1/2" from the front edge of the side (G); they do not cover the dado at the back edge.

12. Repeat Step 11 to attach the remaining three inner supports (I) to the other side (G).

13. Cut two 36"-long shelves (J) from 1 x 12 pine.

14. Install one shelf (J) between the two sides (G) and over the middle inner supports (I), as shown in *Figure 8*, placing the shelf (J) 1-1/2" from the front edges of the sides (G). Glue the shelf (J) in place and insert three 1-1/4" screws through its face and into the edge of each inner support (I). Also insert screws through the side (G) and into the ends of the shelf (J).

15. Repeat Step 14 to attach a second shelf (J) over the lowest pair of inner supports (I), as shown in *Figure 8*.

16. Cut one 36"-long top (K) from 1 x 12 pine.

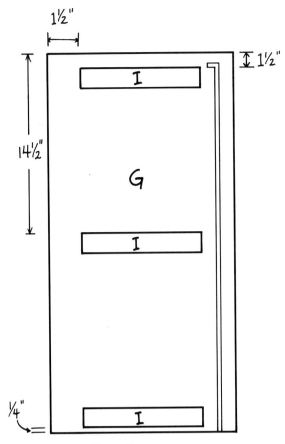

Figure 7

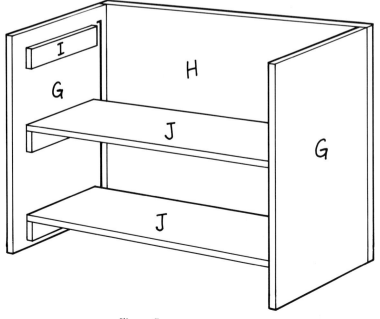

Figure 8

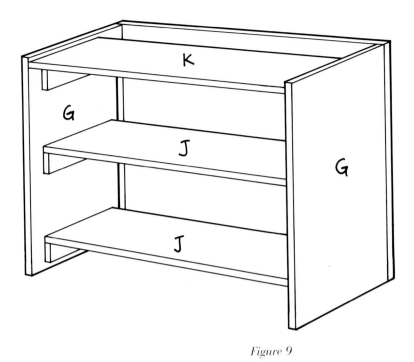

Figure 9

Figure 10

ADDING THE TRIM

1. Cut three 36"-long trim pieces (M) from 1 x 4 pine.

2. Glue one trim piece (M) to the front ends of the upper inner supports (I), between the two sides (G), as shown in *Figure 10*. Secure the trim (M) by driving two 1-1/4" screws through its face and into the end of each inner support (I). Also insert 1-1/4" screws, spaced about 6" apart, through the top (K) and into the trim piece (M).

3. Glue the second and third trim pieces (M) to the two shelves (J) and the front ends of the middle inner supports (I), between the two sides (G), as shown in *Figure 10*. Secure with two 1-1/4" screws inserted through the face of each trim piece (M) and into the inner support (I) at each joint. Also insert 1-1/4" screws, spaced about 6" apart, through each trim piece (M) and into the edge of each shelf (J).

4. Cut one 36"-long bottom trim piece (N) from 1 x 3 pine.

5. Attach the bottom trim piece (N) between the two sides (G), flush with the bottom edge of the lower trim piece (M) and with the bottom of the cabinet, as shown in *Figure 10*. Insert 1-1/4" screws, spaced about 6" apart, to secure the bottom trim piece (N).

INSTALLING THE DESKTOP

1. Turn the completed desk/cabinet upside-down. Fit the assembled desktop, with the desktop front (D) facing down, into the opening in the back of the cabinet, fitting the dowel rods attached to the desktop assembly into the dadoes in the sides (G).

2. Now you'll attach the top support (L) to the top (K). The top support (L) serves to keep the desktop assembly from dropping all the way down into the cabinet when the desktop isn't in use. With the desk/cabinet still upside down, place the top support (L) on the 36"-long edge of the top (K) that is closest to the desktop assembly. Note that the top (K) is 1" longer than the top support (L) at each end. Make certain that the top support (L) overlaps the top (K) by 1-1/2", as shown in *Figure 11*. Then glue the top

17. Cut one 34"-long top support (L) from 1 x 4 pine. Set this piece aside; you'll add it to the top (K) during final assembly.

18. Attach the top (K) over the top inner supports (I), between the two sides (G) and flush with their front edges (see *Figure 9*).

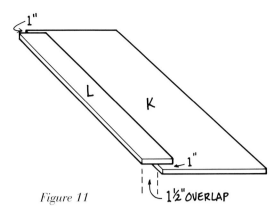

Figure 11

support (L) in place and insert 1-1/4" screws, spaced about 4" apart, through it and into the top (K). Be sure to attach the top support (L) only to the top (K) and not to the desktop front (D).

3. Turn the desk/cabinet right side up.

MAKING THE CABINET DOORS

1. Cut two 25-1/4" x 17-3/4" cabinet doors (O) from laminated pine.

2. Using a router and roundover bit, rout all four edges on what will be the front face of each door (O).

3. Fit the doors (O) into the opening at the front of the desk/cabinet, and check their fit. Then attach two concealed cabinet hinges to each of the doors (O) and to the inside of the desk/cabinet.

FINISHING

1. Using a router and roundover bit, round both edges of the sides (G) and back (H) of the cabinet.

2. Fill all holes, cracks, and crevices with wood filler. Pay particular attention to the routed edges of the back (H) of the cabinet; because it is plywood, it will require more filler than the rest of the cabinet.

3. Sand all surfaces of the desk/cabinet thoroughly.

4. Paint or stain the project the color of your choice.

5. Install recessed drawer pulls on the desktop front (D).

6. Install one cabinet knob on each of the doors (O), being careful to align them with one another.

BUFFET TABLE

This project, shown on page 95, is a versatile piece of furniture that several of my friends have admired. It works well in an entry hall, as a sofa table, or as a buffet in the dining room.

MATERIALS AND SUPPLIES

30 linear feet of 1 x 3 pine

54 linear feet of 1 x 4 pine

4 linear feet of 1 x 6 pine

5 linear feet of 1 x 10 pine

1 piece of laminated pine, 26" x 54"

1 piece of 1/4"-thick plywood, 9" x 15"

Iron-on bonding material

HARDWARE

Approximately 300 #6 x 1-1/4" flathead wood screws

Approximately 35 3d finishing nails

CUTTING LIST

Code	Description	Qty.	Material	Dimensions
A	Shelf	1	Laminated pine	11-1/2" x 50-1/2"
B	Long Shelf Support	2	1 x 4 pine	50-1/2" long
C	Short Shelf Support	2	1 x 4 pine	10" long
D	Long Top Support	4	1 x 3 pine	50-1/2" long
E	Short Top Support	4	1 x 3 pine	10" long
F	Long Guide	6	1 x 4 pine	11-1/2" long
G	Short Guide	6	1 x 4 pine	10" long
H	Leg	8	1 x 4 pine	30" long
I	Back Trim	1	1 x 10 pine	45" long
J	Side Trim	2	1 x 10 pine	4-1/2" long
K	Top/Bottom Trim	2	1 x 3 pine	45" long
L	Vertical Trim	2	1 x 3 pine	4-1/4" long
M	Drawer Front/Back	4	1 x 4 pine	15-1/4" long
N	Drawer Side	4	1 x 4 pine	8" long
O	Drawer Bottom	2	1/4" plywood	8-1/4" x 14"
P	Small Drawer Front/Back	2	1 x 4 pine	8-3/4" long
Q	Small Drawer Side	2	1 x 4 pine	8" long
R	Small Drawer Bottom	1	1/4" plywood	7-1/2" x 8-1/4"
S	Long Drawer Front	2	1 x 6 pine	16-1/2" long
T	Short Drawer Front	1	1 x 6 pine	10" long
U	Table Top	1	Laminated pine	13-1/2" x 54"

NOTES ON MATERIALS

The buffet table top and shelf are constructed of laminated 1 x 4 pine boards. Most building-supply stores sell sections of pine that have already been laminated. You can laminate the boards yourself, of course, but I don't recommend doing so unless you're a very experienced woodworker and own the necessary tools.

Before you decide whether to add fabric cutouts to your finished project, read over the instructions in the "Finishing" section; they'll explain how to add these cutouts and how to estimate the amount of bonding material (available at most fabric stores) you'll need to buy for the fabric you choose.

MAKING THE SHELF

1. Cut one 11-1/2" x 50-1/2" shelf (A) from laminated pine.

2. Cut two long shelf supports (B) from 1 x 4 pine, each measuring 50-1/2" long. Cut two short shelf supports (C) from 1 x 4 pine, each measuring 10" long.

3. Place the two long shelf supports (B) on a level surface, parallel to each other, on edge, and 10" apart. Place the two short shelf supports (C) between the two long shelf supports (B) as shown in *Figure 1*. Glue the supports together and drive two 1-1/4" screws through the long shelf supports (B) into the short shelf supports (C) at each joint.

4. Glue the shelf (A) onto the shelf support assembly, as shown in *Figure 1*. Drive 1-1/4" screws through the top of the shelf (A) into the edges of the shelf-support assembly, spacing the screws about 6" apart.

Making the Support Assemblies

1. Cut four long top supports (D) from 1 x 3 pine, each measuring 50-1/2" long.

2. Cut four short top supports (E) from 1 x 3 pine, each measuring 10" long.

3. Place two of the long top supports (D) on a level surface, parallel to each other, on edge, and 10" apart. Place two short top supports (E) between the two long top supports (D), as shown in *Figure 2*. Glue the supports together and insert two 1-1/4" screws through the long top supports (D) into the short top supports (E) at each joint.

4. Repeat Step 3, using the remaining two long top supports (D) and two short top supports (E) to form a second support assembly. Set the second assembly aside.

5. The support assembly that you built in Step 3 will support the drawers. The next step is to construct the drawer-guide assemblies and add them to the support assembly. Start by cutting six long guides (F) from 1 x 4 pine, each measuring 11-1/2" long. Also cut six short guides (G) from 1 x 4 pine, each measuring 10" long.

6. Glue one short guide (G) to the edge of one long guide (F), as shown in *Figure 3*, leaving a 3/4" space at each end of the long guide (F). Note that the back face of the long guide (F) should be flush with the back edge of the short guide (G). Fasten the pieces with three 1-1/4" screws, spacing them evenly along the joint.

7. Repeat Step 6 five more times, using the remaining five short guides (G) and five long guides (F).

8. Now you'll attach the guide assemblies to the first support assembly, as shown in *Figure 4*. Begin on the left side, placing the first guide assembly with its short guide (G) portion inside the first support assembly and with the outer face of its long guide portion (F) 1-1/4" from the inside edge of the support assembly.

9. Position the second guide assembly so that the two short guide (G) portions of the first and second assemblies are 10" apart.

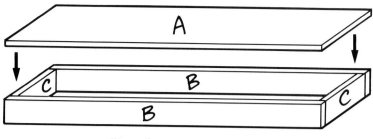

Figure 1

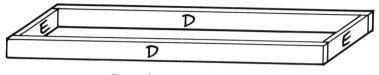

Figure 2

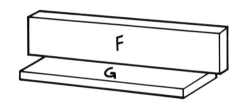

SIDE VIEW

Figure 3

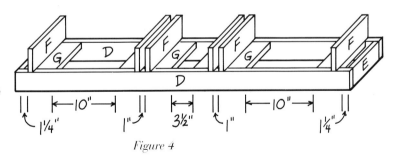

Figure 4

10. Position the third assembly so that the long guide (F) portions of the second and third assemblies are 1" apart.

11. Repeat Steps 8 through 10, working from the right side of the support assembly to attach the remaining guide assemblies, as shown in *Figure 4*.

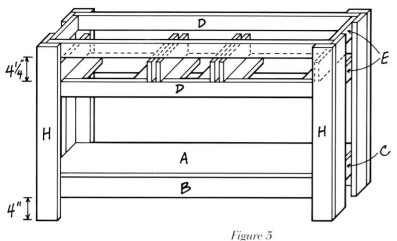

Figure 5

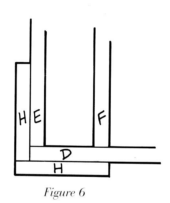

Figure 6

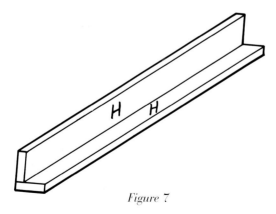

Figure 7

ADDING THE LEGS

1. Cut eight 30"-long legs (H) from 1 x 4 pine. Before assembling the legs, study *Figures 5* and *6* to see how they're attached to both the inner support assemblies and the shelf assembly. The tops of the legs (H) will be flush with the upper edges of the inner support assembly (the one without the drawer guides attached). The inner support assembly with the drawer guides attached will be positioned 4-1/4" below the bottom edge of the first inner support assembly, and the bottom edge of the shelf assembly will be positioned 4" from the bottom of the legs. The front and back legs (H) will overlap the edges of the side legs (H).

Start by gluing two legs (H) together at a 90-degree angle, as shown in *Figure 7*. Secure with 1-1/4" screws spaced about 6" apart along the joint.

2. Repeat the leg-gluing procedure in Step 1 three more times to form the remaining three leg assemblies.

3. Position the assembled legs as shown in *Figures 5* and *6*; then glue them to each of the three center assemblies. Secure with two 1-1/4" screws at each joint.

ADDING THE BACK AND SIDE TRIM

1. Cut one 45"-long back trim (I) from 1 x 10 pine.

2. Glue the back trim (I) between the two back legs (H). Insert 1-1/4" screws through the back trim (I) into the inner support assemblies, spacing the screws about 6" apart.

3. Cut two 4-1/2"-long side trim pieces (J) from 1 x 10 pine.

4. Glue a side trim piece (J) between each set of legs (H) on the sides of the buffet. Insert four 1-1/4" screws through each side trim piece (J) into the inner support assemblies, locating two screws at the top and two at the bottom.

ADDING THE FRONT TRIM

1. Cut two top/bottom trim pieces (K) from 1 x 3 pine, each measuring 45" long.

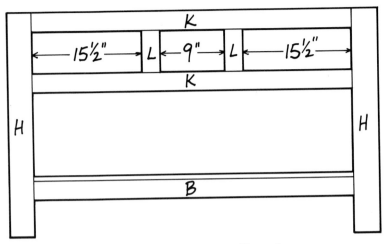

Figure 8

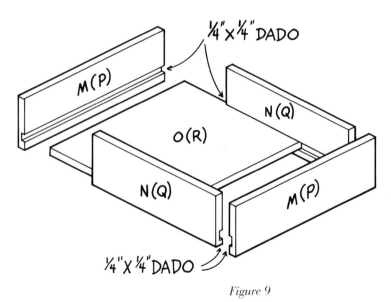

Figure 9

2. Glue one top/bottom trim (K) to the top front of the assembly, over the long top support (D), as shown in *Figure 8*. Secure the trim with 1-1/4" screws spaced about 6" apart.

3. Repeat Step 2 to attach the remaining top/bottom trim (K) to the assembly, over the lower long top support (D).

4. Cut two 4-1/4"-long vertical trim pieces (L) from 1 x 3 pine.

5. Using *Figure 8* as a guide, glue one vertical trim (L) between the two top/bottom pieces (K), 15-1/2" from the left leg (H). Insert two 1-1/4" screws through the vertical trim (L) into the ends of the long drawer guides (F).

6. Repeat Step 5 to attach the remaining vertical trim (L) on the right side, as shown in *Figure 8*. This will leave a 9"-wide opening between the two vertical trim pieces (L).

Making the Drawers

1. The two outermost drawers in the buffet are identical in size; the center drawer is smaller. All three are constructed as shown in the assembly diagram in *Figure 9*. Start by cutting the following parts for the two larger drawers from 1 x 4 pine: four drawer front/back pieces (M), each 15-1/4" long, and four drawer sides (N), each 8" long.

2. To accommodate the plywood drawer bottoms, cut a 1/4" x 1/4" dado on the inside of each drawer piece (M and N), 3/8" from the lower edge.

3. Cut two 8-1/4" x 14" drawer bottoms (O) from 1/4"-thick plywood. Assemble one drawer as shown in *Figure 9*. Note that the drawer front/back pieces (M) overlap the ends of the drawer sides (N). Use glue and 3d finishing nails at each end of the overlapping boards. The long drawer front (S) will be added later.

4. Repeat the drawer assembly using the remaining two drawer front/back pieces (M), two drawer sides (N), and drawer bottom (O)

5. Cut the following pieces for the center drawer: two 8-3/4"-long small drawer front/back pieces (P) and two 8"-long small drawer side pieces (Q).

6. Cut one 7-1/2" x 8-1/4" small drawer bottom (R) from 1/4"-thick plywood. Assemble the drawer as shown in *Figure 9*. Note that the small drawer/front back pieces (P) overlap the ends of the small drawer sides (Q). Again, use glue and 3d finishing nails on each end of the overlapping boards.

MAKING THE DRAWER FRONTS

1. Cut two long drawer fronts (S) from 1 x 6 pine, each measuring 16-1/2" long.

2. Cut one short drawer front (T) from 1 x 6 pine, measuring 10" long.

3. To attach the drawer fronts (S and T) to the assembled drawers, set each of the drawers inside their respective drawer openings, on top of the drawer guides. Place a piece of wood between the back of each drawer and the back of the buffet so that the drawers are held flush with the front of the buffet. Use heavy-duty, double-sided tape to hold a drawer front temporarily in place on each drawer until you have all three drawer fronts positioned exactly right. The drawer fronts should be level with each other, and the spacing should be equal on both sides of the center drawer. Then attach the fronts to the drawers. Insert three 1-1/4" screws through each drawer and into the drawer front.

ADDING THE TOP

1. Cut one 13-1/2" x 54" top (U) from the remaining laminated pine.

2. Center the top (U) over the completed buffet assembly and glue it in place. Then insert 1-1/4" screws, spaced about 8" apart, through the top (U) and into the buffet assembly.

FINISHING

1. Fill any screw holes with wood filler.

2. Sand all surfaces thoroughly.

3. Paint or stain the completed buffet the color of your choice. We used a lavender paint for our project.

4. If you don't plan to add the fabric cutouts to your project, skip down to Step 8. To add some visual interest to our project and to repeat the fabric design in our living room, I added fabric cutouts to the front and one side of the buffet. The method is time-consuming, but not at all difficult. First, decide what portion of your fabric design you want to transfer to the buffet. Large designs are easier to work with because each portion must be cut out by hand.

5. Following the manufacturer's instructions, iron the chosen section of fabric to one side of the bonding material. The attached bonding material will make the fabric stiff enough to enable you to cut around the designs without the edges raveling. Use small sharp scissors to carefully cut out the designs.

6. Lay the cutout over the painted buffet, positioning it as desired. Then remove the backing on the bonding material, and following the manufacturer's instructions, iron the designs onto the buffet.

7. In order to create a smooth finished surface, you will need to apply several coats of varnish over the fabric. The number of coats will vary with the thickness of your particular fabric. I used a product that's advertised as the equivalent of over 50 coats of varnish; it worked well and was a big time-saver!

8. Install the drawer pulls according to the manufacturer's instructions, centering one on the front of each drawer.

CHAISE LOUNGE

I wanted a comfortable retreat in my bed-room where I could read quietly or watch television. But anyone who has priced chaise lounges in furniture stores knows why I kept putting off the purchase. Eventually, I decided to make my own chaise, and here's the result! I now have my own little corner of the world—at a reasonable price.

SPECIAL TECHNIQUES

Beveling

MATERIALS AND SUPPLIES

65 linear feet of 2 x 4 pine

1 sheet of 3/4"-thick plywood, 4' x 8'

15 yards of 36"-wide fabric

8 bags of polyester fiberfill

1 piece 2"-thick foam, 14" x 50"

1 piece 2"-thick foam, 28" x 45-1/2"

HARDWARE

Approximately 20 #6 x 2" flathead wood screws

Approximately 200 #6 x 2-1/2" flathead wood screws

Approximately 10 3d finishing nails

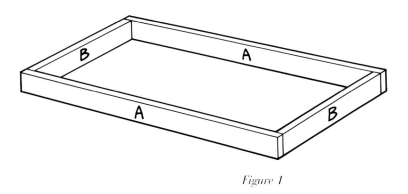

Figure 1

CUTTING LIST

Code	Description	Qty.	Material	Dimensions
A	Long Frame	4	2 x 4 pine	54" long
B	Short Frame	4	2 x 4 pine	25" long
C	Short Connector	2	2 x 4 pine	19" long
D	Long Connector	4	2 x 4 pine	31" long
E	Top Side	2	2 x 4 pine	20" long
F	Top Back	1	2 x 4 pine	28" long
G	Arm Connector	2	2 x 4 pine	8-1/2" long
H	Side Connector	4	2 x 4 pine	13" long
I	Short Seat Support	2	2 x 4 pine	22" long
J	Long Seat Support	2	2 x 4 pine	25" long
K	Back	1	3/4" plywood	13-7/8" x 22"
L	Seat	1	3/4" plywood	See *Fig. 9*

MAKING THE LOWER FRAME

1. The lower portion of the inner frame consists of an upper and lower support and is constructed entirely of 2 x 4 pine. To make the lower support, begin by cutting two long frames (A), each measuring 54" long, and two short frames (B), each measuring 25" long.

2. Place the two long frames (A) on a level surface, parallel to each other, on edge, and 25" apart. Fit the two short frames (B) between the ends of the long frames (A) to form a rectangle measuring 28" x 54", as shown in *Figure 1*. Glue the pieces together and insert two 2-1/2" screws through each long frame (A) and into the end of each short frame (B) at each joint.

3. Repeat Steps 1 and 2 to make a 28" x 54" upper support.

4. The upper and lower supports are joined by 2 x 4 pine connectors (C and D). Cut two short connectors (C), each 19" long, and four long connectors (D), each 31" long.

5. Place the lower support on a level surface and glue the two short connectors (C) inside adjacent corners of the lower

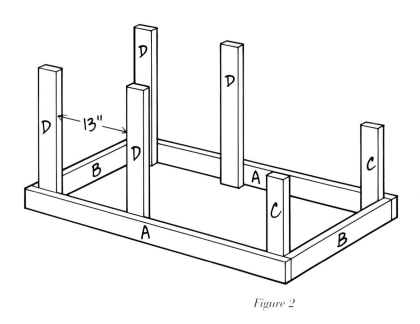

Figure 2

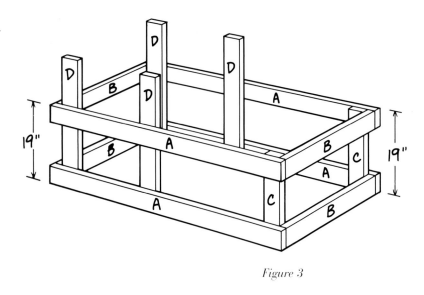

Figure 3

support, as shown in *Figure 2*. Insert two 2-1/2" screws, one through each long frame (A) and one through each short frame (B) into each short connector (C).

6. Glue two of the long connectors (D) in the opposite corners of the lower support, as shown in *Figure 2*. Insert two 2-1/2" screws, one through each long frame (A) and one through each short frame (B) at each joint.

7. Glue the remaining two long connectors (D) to the lower support, placing each one 13" from the long connector (D) on that side, as shown in *Figure 2*. Secure with two 2-1/2" screws driven through each long connector (D) and into the lower support at each joint.

8. The next step is to add the upper support to the assembly, as shown in *Figure 3*. Carefully fit the upper support over the long and short connectors (C and D). The upper support should be flush with the ends of the short connectors (C) and should be perfectly level. Glue the upper support in place and secure it with two 2-1/2" screws driven through the long or short support (A or B) at each joint.

ADDING THE TOP FRAME PIECES

1. Cut two 20"-long top sides (E) from 2 x 4 pine.

2. Glue the top sides (E) to the outer surfaces of the long connectors (D), as shown in *Figure 4*. Insert two 2-1/2" screws at each joint.

3. Cut one 28"-long top back (F) from 2 x 4 pine.

4. Glue the top back (F) to the ends of the top sides (E) and edges of the long connectors (D), as shown in *Figure 4*. Insert two 2-1/2" screws at each joint.

5. Cut two 8-1/2"-long arm connectors (G) from 2 x 4 pine.

6. Glue the arm connectors (G) between the top sides (E) and the long frames (A) in the upper supports, as shown in *Figure 4*. Insert two 2-1/2" screws at each end of each arm connector (G).

7. Cut four 13"-long side connectors (H) from 2 x 4 pine.

8. Cut two short seat supports (I), each measuring 22" long, from 2 x 4 pine.

9. Place two of the side connectors (H) on a level surface, parallel, on edge, and 22" apart. Place the two short seat supports (I) face down, at opposite ends of the two side connectors (H), as shown in *Figure 5*.

10. Glue the side connectors (H) to the short seat supports (I) and secure with 2-1/2" screws inserted through the side connectors (H) and into the ends of the short seat supports (I).

11. Fit the assembly (H and I) inside the upper support, as shown in *Figure 6*, so that the two side connectors (H) are flush against the inner faces of the upper support between the two long connectors (D). Glue the assembly in place and insert three 2-1/2" screws through each side of the upper support and into each side connector (H).

12. Glue the remaining two side connectors (H) to the inner faces of the top sides (E), between the two long supports (D), as shown in *Figure 6*. Insert three 2-1/2" screws through each side connector (H) and into each top side (E).

13. Cut two long seat supports (J) from 2 x 4 pine, each 25" long.

14. Attach one long seat support (J), face up, inside the upper support, next to the two short connectors (C), as shown in *Figure 6*. Glue the long seat support (J) in place and insert two 2-1/2" screws through each side of the upper support at each joint.

Repeat to attach the second long seat support (J) inside the upper support, flush with the edges of the two long connectors (D), as shown in *Figure 6*.

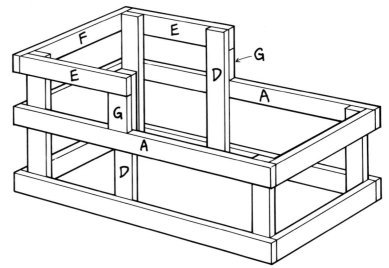

Figure 4

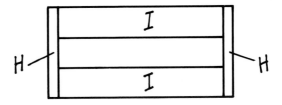

Figure 5

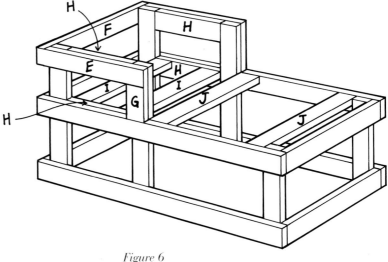

Figure 6

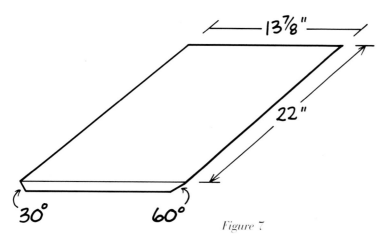

Figure 7

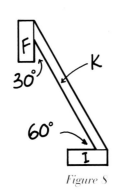

Figure 8

of foam extends outward from each side of the back (K). Staple the foam to the front face of the back, placing just one staple in each of the corners to hold the foam temporarily. Fill the resulting depressions in the foam with a small amount of polyester fiberfill. Push the foam that extends from the sides of the back (K) into the cavities formed by the two long connectors (D) behind the back.

4. Using *Figure 9* as a guide, cut a seat (L) from 3/4"-thick plywood.

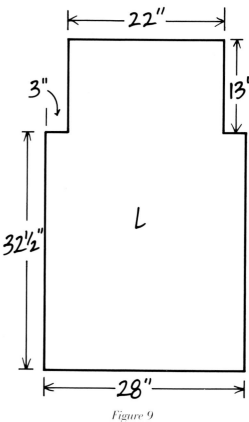

Figure 9

CONSTRUCTING THE BACK AND SEAT

1. Cut a 13-7/8" x 22" back piece (K) from 3/4"-thick plywood. Bevel one 22" edge at a 30-degree angle and the other at a 60-degree angle, as shown in *Figure 7*.

2. Glue the beveled edges of the back (K) to the top back (F) and the front of the short seat support (I) closest to the top back (F), as shown in *Figure 8*. Secure the back (K) with four evenly spaced finishing nails driven through the 22"-long edge.

3. Cut a 14" x 50" piece of 2"-thick foam. Center the 53" length across the front face of the back (K), so that approximately 14"

5. Cut a piece of 2"-thick foam to match the dimensions of the plywood seat (L).

6. Staple the matching foam to the plywood seat (L) in three or four places to hold it in place temporarily. Fill the resulting depressions with a small amount of polyester fiberfill.

7. Cut a piece of fabric that is 4" larger than the seat (L) on all sides.

8. Place the fabric on a smooth surface, right side down. Center the seat (L), foam side down, on top of the fabric. Wrap the fabric over the edges of the seat (L) and staple it to the plywood. To minimize wrinkles, first staple the center of one side, then the center of the opposite side, and then work your way out to the corners, smoothing the fabric as you go. Staple the centers of the remaining sides and again work your way to the corners. Be generous with the staples; use enough to keep the fabric taut and to eliminate puckering.

ADDING THE FABRIC TO THE FRAME

1. Cut six 24"-long pieces of fabric, each 36" wide, and seam them together at the sides to form a long rectangle, approximately 6 yards wide and 24" long, as shown in *Figure 10*.

2. Sew two lines of gathering stitches on each of the 6-yard-long edges, as shown in *Figure 10*. Pull the gathers until the fabric measures 98" long on both the top and bottom edges.

3. This gathered piece of fabric will be used to cover the area between the upper and lower supports at the end of the chaise where you place your feet. Beginning just behind one of the middle long connectors (D), staple the fabric to the top of the long frame (A). Pull it down tightly and staple the other gathered edge to the bottom edge of the lower support. Continue working around the side, across the front, and down the other side, alternately stapling at the top and bottom. End just behind the opposite long connector (D).

4. Cut four 35"-long pieces of fabric, each 36" wide, and seam them together at the sides to form a rectangle about 4 yards long and 35" wide.

5. Sew two lines of gathering stitches on each of the 4-yard-long edges. Pull the gathers until the fabric measures 72" long on both the top and bottom edges.

6. This second gathered piece of fabric will be used to cover the area between the top frame and the lower support on the back and sides of the chaise lounge. Fold under a 1"-edge and begin just at the front edge of the long connector (D). Staple the fabric to the top of the top side (E). Pull the fabric down tightly and staple the other gathered edge to the bottom edge of the lower support. Continue working around the side, across the back, and along the other side, alternately stapling at the top and bottom. End just at the front edge of the opposite long connector (D), folding over the final raw edge of the fabric at the end.

7. Cut two 20"-long pieces of fabric, each 36" wide. These will be used to cover the fronts of the arms.

8. On one fabric width, sew two lines of gathering stitches on each of the 36" edges. Pull the gathers until the fabric measures 16" long on both the top and bottom edges.

9. Fold under a 1" edge on one 20" side of the fabric. Then staple the 16" gathered fabric edge, with the fabric's right side facing the chaise, along the inner edge of the

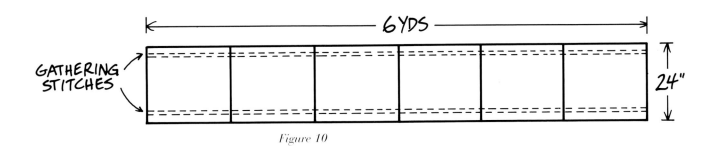

GATHERING STITCHES

6 YDS

24"

Figure 10

arm connector (G), starting at the bottom rear, where the arm connector (G) meets the upper support. Fold over the final raw edge at the end.

10. The next step is to pad the arm (D and G). This is easy to do, but may require a few trial-and-error efforts to find out just how much fiberfill to use and to distribute it evenly over the arm. Cover the arm with a generous amount of fiberfill. Then pull the fabric, with its right side up, over the fiberfill to cover the opposite side and the top front of the arm. Finding a helper to hold the fabric in place while you evaluate your work will make your life easier. Adjust the amount of fiberfill, if necessary. When you're satisfied with the way the arm looks, staple the other gathered edge of the fabric to the inner edge of the arm connector (G) and the side connector (H). Adjust the gathers evenly along the arm.

11. Repeat Steps 9 and 10 to pad the remaining arm and cover it with fabric.

12. Now you're on the home stretch! Cut four 34"-long fabric widths. Seam them together to form a rectangle 4 yards long x 34" wide. This will be used to cover the rest of the arms and the back (E, F, and H).

13. Sew two lines of gathering stitches on each of the 4-yard-long edges. Pull the gathers until the fabric measures 72" long on both the top and bottom edges.

14. Fold under a 1" edge and begin at the lower edge of the top side (E) where it meets the back edge of the arm connector (G). Place the fabric right side up against the chaise, so that the gathering stitches are along the lower edge of the top side (E). Staple the fabric to the lower edge of the top side (E) and then work your way around, stapling the fabric along the lower edge of the top back (F) and the lower edge of the opposite top side (E), ending directly opposite to where you started. Fold over the final raw edge at the end.

15. The next step is to pad the arms and back (E, F, and H). Follow the same procedure outlined in Step 10, covering the arms and back with a generous amount of fiberfill, pulling the fabric over the fiberfill

to cover the arms and back, and stapling the gathered edge to the bottom edges of the side connectors (H) and to the bottom edge of the plywood back (K). Adjust the gathers evenly along the arms and back.

FINISHING

1. Install the padded seat (L) over the upper support. Insert three 2" screws through each seat support (I and J) into the padded seat (L).

2. Find your favorite book or magazine, throw a couple of pillows and a quilt on your chaise, and take a breather.

RUSTIC ARMOIRE

Most of my favorite project designs result from satisfying my own needs. The one shown on the next page is no exception. I designed and built this armoire to fit in a small room in our house that was designated by the builder to be a "study." He must have pictured the future owners installing floor-to-ceiling bookshelves, a massive globe, and leather-covered easy chairs. What I needed, however, was a guest room—ahh, reality! The problem was that the room had no closet and not much space left over when the sleeper sofa was open for guests. This armoire neatly solved both of my problems. Although it's only 12" deep, it has a small hanging closet for clothes and enough drawer space to accommodate guests' necessities. Because the armoire is so narrow, it must be attached to the wall to provide stability when the doors and/or drawers are open.

SPECIAL TECHNIQUES

Mitering

Dadoes

Ripping

MATERIALS AND SUPPLIES

80 linear feet of 3/4" x 3/4" pine

44 linear feet of 1 x 3 pine

37 linear feet of 1 x 4 pine

13 linear feet of 1 x 6 pine

15 linear feet of 1 x 8 pine

33 linear feet of 1 x 12 pine

2 pieces of laminated pine or oak, each 20" x 72"

1 piece of 1/4"-thick plywood, 20" x 34"

2 sheets of 3/4"-thick plywood, each 4' x 8'

10 linear feet of 5" crown molding

CUTTING LIST

Code	Description	Qty.	Material	Dimensions
A	Wide Back	1	3/4" plywood	41-1/8" x 70-1/2"
B	Narrow Back	1	3/4" plywood	23-1/8" x 70-1/2"
C	Inner Vertical Support	8	3/4" x 3/4" pine	70-1/2" long
D	Shelf Support	3	3/4" x 3/4" pine	39-5/8" long
E	Side	2	1 x 12 pine	72" long
F	Inner Divider	1	1 x 12 pine	70-1/2" long
G	Top/Bottom	2	1 x 12 pine	65" long
H	Narrow Front Vertical	2	1 x 4 pine	72" long
I	Center Front Vertical	1	1 x 6 pine	72" long
J	Narrow Horizontal Frame	2	1 x 4 pine	36" long
K	Short Horizontal Frame	2	1 x 4 pine	18" long
L	Horizontal Inner Support	4	3/4" x 3/4" pine	39-5/8" long
M	Shelf	1	1 x 12 pine, ripped	41-1/8" long
N	Wide Horizontal Frame	2	1 x 6 pine	36" long
O	Short Inner Support	4	3/4" x 3/4" pine	21-5/8" long
P	Drawer Front/Back	4	1 x 8 pine	35" long
Q	Drawer Side	4	1 x 8 pine	9" long
R	Drawer Bottom	2	1/4" plywood	9-3/8" x 33-7/8"
S	Drawer Front	2	Laminated pine	8-1/2" x 35-1/2"
T	Top/Bottom Trim	4	1 x 3 pine	33" long
U	Side Trim	4	1 x 3 pine	11" long
V1	Upper Drawer Guide	4	1 x 4 pine	10-1/2" long
V2	Lower Drawer Guide	4	1 x 4 pine	9" long
W	Cabinet Door	2	Laminated pine	17-1/2" x 35-1/2"
X	Top/Bottom Door Trim	4	1 x 3 pine	15-1/4" long
Y	Side Door Trim	3	1 x 3 pine	37-1/2" long
Z	Wardrobe Door	1	Laminated pine	17-1/2" x 64"
AA	Top/Bottom Wardrobe Door Trim	2	1 x 3 pine	15" long
BB	Side Wardrobe Door Trim	2	1 x 3 pine	66-1/4" long
CC	Top Side Trim	2	1 x 4 pine	12" long
DD	Top Front Trim	1	1 x 4 pine	68" long

HARDWARE

2 lbs. #6 x 1-1/4" flathead wood screws

1 lb. #6 x 2" flathead wood screws

Approximately 50 2d finishing nails

Approximately 200 3d finishing nails

6 offset door hinges

7 drawer pulls

NOTES ON MATERIALS

The armoire drawers and doors shown here are constructed from laminated pine boards. Most building-supply stores sell sections of wood that have already been laminated. You can laminate the boards yourself, of course, but I don't recommend doing this unless you're an experienced woodworker and own heavy-duty tools. Due to the number of boards and the overall size of the project, laminating is a bigger job than it may appear to be.

Although this armoire isn't wide enough to accommodate clothes hangers suspended parallel to its sides, you can certainly hang clothes parallel to its front and back. Just purchase a wooden towel rod with removable arms, attach the arms to the inside top of the armoire, and cut the rod down to a length that will fit between the arms.

CONSTRUCTING THE BACK

1. The basic supporting frame for the armoire is nothing more than a large box. Although it requires quite a bit of space to construct, the actual assembly is very straightforward. Start by cutting one 41-1/8" x 70-1/2" wide back (A) and one 23-1/8" x 70-1/2" narrow back (B) from the 3/4"-thick plywood.

2. Cut eight 70-1/2"-long inner vertical supports (C) from 3/4" x 3/4" pine.

3. Using *Figure 1* as a guide, glue two inner vertical supports (C) to the wide back (A), positioning the supports flush with the long edges of the wide back (A). Use 3d finishing nails, spaced about 6" apart, to secure the supports in place.

4. Cut three 39-5/8"-long shelf supports (D) from 3/4" x 3/4" pine.

5. Glue one shelf support (D) to the wide back (A), between the two vertical supports (C) and 39-3/4" down from what will be the top of the finished armoire, as shown in *Figure 1*. Secure the shelf sup-

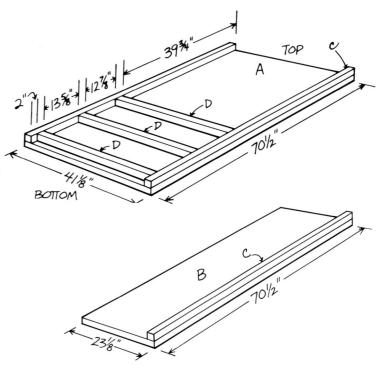

Figure 1

port with 3d finishing nails, spaced about 6" apart. It doesn't make any difference which end of the wide back (A) you choose as the top, but now is the time to decide.

6. Glue a second shelf support (D) to the wide back (A), 12-7/8" down from the first support, in the same manner that you attached the first one, as shown in *Figure 1*.

7. Nail and glue the remaining shelf support (D) 2" from the bottom edge of the wide back (A).

8. Glue and nail one inner vertical support (C) to the narrow back (B), flush with one long edge, as shown in *Figure 1*. Secure the support with 3d finishing nails spaced about 6" apart.

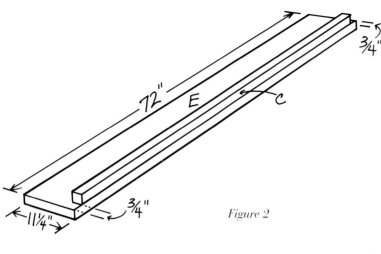

Figure 2

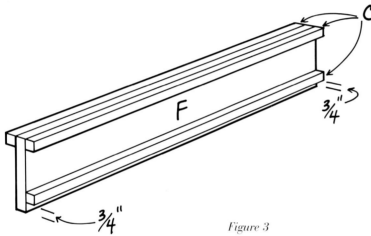

Figure 3

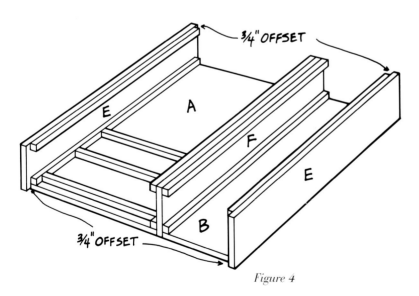

Figure 4

Adding the Sides and Inner Divider

1. Cut two 72"-long sides (E) from 1 x 12 pine.

2. Glue one inner vertical support (C) flush with one 70-1/2"-long edge of one side (E), as shown in *Figure 2*. Center the inner vertical support (C), leaving a 3/4" gap at each end of the side (E). Secure the support with 3d finishing nails, spaced about 6" apart.

3. Repeat Step 2 to attach another inner vertical support (C) to the remaining side (E).

4. Cut one 70-1/2" long inner divider (F) from 1 x 12 pine.

5. Glue an inner vertical support (C) to each side of the inner divider (F), flush with one edge, as shown in *Figure 3*. Secure with 3d finishing nails spaced about 6" apart.

6. Glue a third inner vertical support (C) to the inner divider (F), offsetting it 3/4" from the other long edge, as shown in *Figure 3*. Secure the support with 3d finishing nails spaced about 6" apart.

7. Place the inner divider (F) along the edge of the wide back assembly, facing its offset inner vertical support (C) away from the wide back (A), as shown in *Figure 4*. Glue the inner divider (F) and wide back assembly together. Then insert 2" screws at an angle through the bottom 3/4"-wide offset on the inner divider (F) and into the inner vertical support (C) that is attached to the wide back (A). Space the screws about 4" apart.

8. Fit the narrow back (B) underneath the offset inner vertical support (C) on the inner divider (F), as shown in *Figure 4*. Glue the narrow back in place and insert 1-1/4" screws, spaced about 4" apart, through the inner vertical support (C) on the inner divider (F) and into the narrow back (B).

9. Center one side (E) on the wide back (A), leaving a 3/4" gap at each end, as shown in *Figure 4*. Glue the side (E) in place and insert screws, spaced about 4" apart, through the side (E) to attach it alternately to both the inner vertical support (C) and to the edge of the wide back (A). Use 2" screws to attach it to the wide back (A) and 1-1/4" screws to attach it to the inner vertical support (C).

10. Center the remaining side (E) along the edge of the narrow back (B), leaving a 3/4" gap at each end, as shown in *Figure 4*. Glue the side in place and secure with screws, just as you secured the side (E) in Step 9.

ADDING THE TOP AND BOTTOM

1. Cut two top/bottom pieces (G) from 1 x 12 pine, each measuring 65" long.

2. Fit one top/bottom piece (G) between the two sides (E), as shown in *Figure 5*. Note that the top/bottom piece (G) fits over the ends of the wide and narrow backs (A and B) and the inner divider (F). Glue the top (G) in place and insert 2" screws, spaced about 3" apart, through the sides (E) and into the ends of the top/bottom piece (G). Also attach the top/bottom piece (G) to the inner divider (F) and to the wide and narrow backs (A and B) by inserting 2" screws, spaced about 3" apart, through the top piece (G) and into the ends of pieces A, B, and F.

3. Repeat Step 2 to attach the other top/bottom piece (G) at the other end of the assembly, as shown in *Figure 5*.

ADDING THE FRONT FRAME PIECES

1. The front frame pieces are not difficult to add, but do take the time to make certain that all the pieces are absolutely square. One piece of the frame that is off will affect the way the shelves and drawers fit, so before you attach each piece, double-check your work. Start by cutting two 72"-long narrow front verticals (H) from 1 x 4 pine.

2. Glue the narrow front verticals (H) to the frame assembly, fitting them over the edges of the sides (E) and the top/bottom pieces (G), as shown in *Figure 6*. Insert 2" screws, spaced about 4" apart, through each narrow front vertical (H) and into the edges of the sides (E) and top/bottom pieces (G).

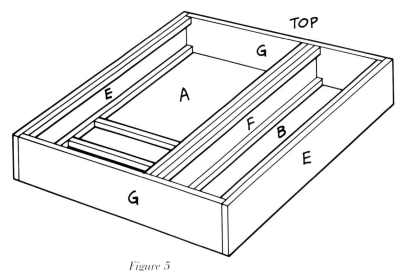

Figure 5

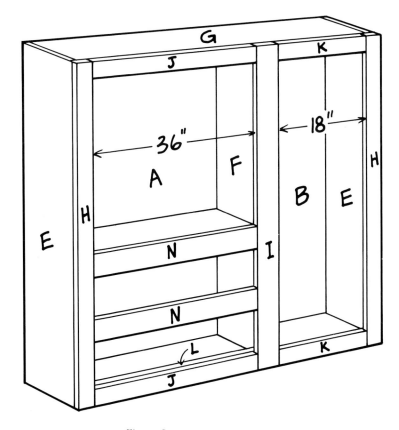

Figure 6

3. Cut one 72"-long center front vertical (I) from 1 x 6 pine.

4. Center the center front vertical (I) over the edge of the inner divider (F). It should extend 2-3/8" on either side of the inner divider (F). At this point, check the spacing on the front of your armoire. (Well, it's almost an armoire by now!) The distance between the center front vertical (I) and the narrow front vertical (H) on the side of the armoire that contains the wide back (A) should be exactly 36". The distance between the center front vertical (I) and the narrow front vertical (H) on the other side of the armoire should be exactly 18". Measure across each of the openings at the top, bottom, and at least two midpoints. If your measurements are off, alter the remaining front frame pieces, drawers, and doors so that they'll fit properly.

5. Cut two 36"-long narrow horizontal frames (J) from 1 x 4 pine.

6. Glue one narrow horizontal frame (J) at the top of the 36"-wide opening on the left side of the armoire, between the center front vertical (I) and the narrow front vertical (H), as shown in *Figure 6*. Insert 2" screws, spaced about 4" apart, through the narrow horizontal frame (J) and into the edge of the top (G).

7. Repeat Step 7 to attach the remaining narrow horizontal frame (J) at the bottom of the 36"-wide opening, as shown in *Figure 6*.

8. Cut two 18"-long short horizontal frames (K) from 1 x 4 pine.

9. Glue one short horizontal frame (K) at the top of the 18"-wide opening on the right side of the armoire, between the center front vertical (I) and the narrow front vertical (H), as shown in *Figure 6*. Insert 2" screws through the short horizontal frame (K) and into the edge of the top (G).

10. Repeat Step 10 to attach the remaining short horizontal frame (K) at the bottom of the 18"-wide opening on the right side of the armoire, as shown in *Figure 6*.

ADDING THE INNER SUPPORTS AND SHELVES

1. Cut four 39-5/8" horizontal inner supports (L) from 3/4" x 3/4" pine. These will fit behind the narrow and wide horizontal frames (J and N) and will support the inner shelves as well as stabilizing the narrow horizontal frames (J) which you just attached. A cutaway view of the placement of the inner supports on the left side of the armoire is provided in *Figure 7*.

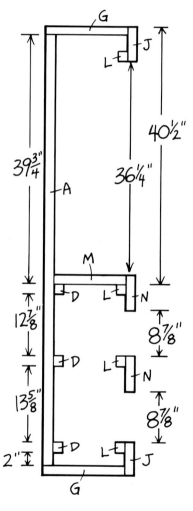

Figure 7

2. Glue one horizontal inner support (L) onto the inner edge of each of the narrow horizontal frame pieces (J), positioning them as shown in *Figure 7*. Secure the supports with 3d finishing nails, spaced about 6" apart.

3. Attach a third horizontal inner support (L) 40-1/2" from the top edge of the armoire, across the front opening. It should be exactly level with the shelf support (D) which you previously attached to the wide back (A). Use 3d finishing nails to secure it to the back faces of the narrow front vertical (H) and the center front vertical (I).

4. Cut one 41-1/8" upper shelf (M) from 1 x 12 pine, and rip the shelf to 10-1/2" in width. The shelf will fit on top of the horizontal inner support (L) which you just attached and the shelf support (D) on the wide back (A), as shown in *Figure 7*. In order to make the shelf fit, each of the corners must be cut out to accommodate the inner vertical supports (C) inside the armoire. Cut out a square from each corner of the upper shelf (M), measuring just over 3/4" x 3/4", as shown in *Figure 8*.

5. Fit the upper shelf (M) over the horizontal inner support (L) and the shelf support (D). Glue the shelf in place, and secure with 3d finishing nails spaced about 6" apart.

6. Cut two 36"-long wide horizontal frames (N) from 1 x 6 pine.

7. Glue one wide horizontal frame (N) over the raw edge of the upper shelf (M), between the center front vertical (I) and the narrow front vertical (H), as shown in *Figures 6* and *7*. Insert 1-1/4" screws, spaced about 6" apart, through the face of the wide horizontal frame (N) and into the edge of the upper shelf (M).

8. We're finally going to use that fourth horizontal inner support (L) that you've been so worried about! Bet you thought we forgot. Attach this support (L) across the 36"-wide opening, 12-7/8" below the horizontal inner support (L) that is under the upper shelf (M), as shown in *Figure 7*. Nail and glue the support (L) to the inner faces of the center front vertical (I) and the narrow front vertical (H).

9. Glue the remaining wide horizontal frame (N) to the horizontal inner support (L) which you just attached. The long upper edge of the wide horizontal frame (N) should be flush with the top edge of the horizontal inner support (L).

10. Cut four 21-5/8"-long short inner supports (O) from 3/4" x 3/4" pine. These will fit behind each of the short horizontal frames (K) on the right side of the armoire to stabilize the joints.

11. Glue and nail one short inner support (O) to the inner face of the short horizontal frame piece (K) at the top of the armoire, flush with its edge. Secure the support with 3d finishing nails spaced about 6" apart.

12. Repeat Step 11 to attach the second short inner support (O) to the short horizontal frame piece (K) at the bottom of the armoire.

MAKING THE DRAWERS

1. There are two identical drawers in this armoire. Both are constructed as shown in *Figure 9*. Start by cutting the following parts from 1 x 8 pine: two 35"-long drawer front/back pieces (P) and two 9"-long drawer sides (Q).

2. To accommodate the plywood drawer bottoms, cut a 1/4" x 1/4" dado on the inside of each drawer piece (P and Q), 3/8" from its lower edge.

Figure 8

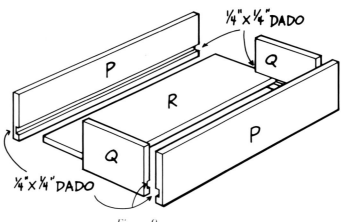

Figure 9

111

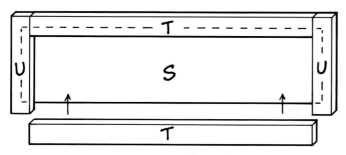

Figure 10

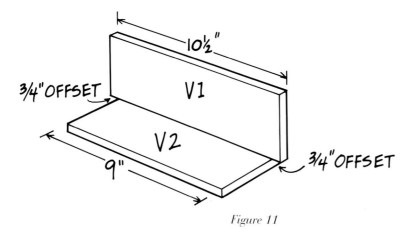

Figure 11

DRAWER OPENING

DRAWER

DRAWER GLIDE

Figure 12

3. Cut two 9-3/8" x 33-7/8" drawer bottoms (R) from 1/4"-thick plywood. Assemble each drawer as shown in *Figure 9*. Note that the drawer front/back pieces (P) overlap the ends of the drawer sides (Q). Use glue and 3d finishing nails at each end of the overlapping boards; leave the drawer bottoms (R) floating freely within their dadoes. The drawer fronts (S) will be added later.

MAKING THE DRAWER FRONTS

1. The drawer fronts are nothing more than rectangles of laminated pine trimmed with a border of 1 x 3 pine. You'll need to make sure that each finished assembly is perfectly square. Start by cutting one 8-1/2" x 35-1/2" drawer front (S) from laminated pine.

2. Cut two 33"-long top/bottom trim pieces (T) from 1 x 3 pine.

3. Cut two 11"-long side trim pieces (U) from 1 x 3 pine.

4. Using *Figure 10* as a guide, place the four trim pieces (T and U) on a level surface. Center the drawer front (S) over the trim pieces, leaving a 1-1/4" border of trim visible on each of the four sides of the drawer front (S). Glue and nail the pieces together, using 3d finishing nails spaced about 4" apart.

5. Repeat Steps 1 through 4 to assemble the second drawer front. Set the drawer fronts aside.

ADDING THE DRAWER GUIDES

1. Cut four 10-1/2"-long upper drawer guides (V1) from 1 x 4 pine. Also cut four 9"-long lower drawer guides (V2) from 1 x 4 pine.

2. Glue one upper guide (V1) and one lower guide (V2) together, as shown in *Figure 11*, leaving a 3/4" space at each end of the upper guide. Note that the back face of the upper guide should be flush with the back edge of the lower guide. Secure the pieces with three 1-1/4"-long screws spaced evenly along the joint.

3. Repeat Step 2 three more times, using the remaining six drawer guide pieces (V1 and V2), to make a total of four assembled drawer guides.

4. Fit the first two L-shaped drawer guides between the horizontal inner support (L) and the shelf support (D) on the sides of the drawer opening, with their open sides facing each other and positioned so that the drawer is centered, as shown in *Figure 12*. Check to make certain that the drawer fits snugly between them. Remove the drawer; then glue and nail the guides in place.

5. Repeat Step 4 to attach the remaining two drawer guides in the second opening.

Making the Cabinet Doors

1. The cabinet doors are constructed in the same manner as the drawer fronts, with the exception that the right-hand cabinet drawer has no trim on the edge that sits next to the left-hand door. Start by cutting two 17-1/2" x 35-1/2" cabinet doors (W) from laminated pine.

2. Cut four 15-1/4"-long top/bottom door trim pieces (X) from 1 x 3 pine.

3. Cut three 37-1/2"-long side door trim pieces (Y) from 1 x 3 pine.

4. Using *Figure 13* as a guide, arrange the five trim pieces (X and Y) on a level surface. (Note the 1/4" gap between the Y piece in the center and X pieces to the right of it.) Center the two door fronts (W) over the trim pieces, leaving a 1/2" gap between the two. There should be a 1-3/8" border of trim visible along each side of the doors (W) and a 1" border at the top and bottom. Glue and nail the door (W) on the left to the trim (X and Y) that it covers, using 3d finishing nails spaced about 4" apart. Glue and nail the door on the right to the two top/bottom trim pieces (X) and to the side door trim piece (Y) on the right, but do not attach this door to the piece of Y trim in the center.

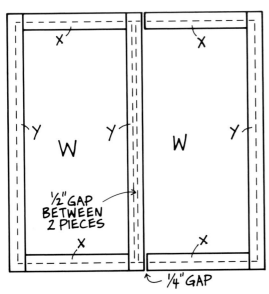

Figure 13

Making the Wardrobe Door

1. The wardrobe door is made in the same manner as the drawer fronts and the cabinet doors; only the measurements are different. Start by cutting one 17-1/2" x 64" wardrobe door (Z) from laminated pine.

2. Cut two 15"-long top/bottom wardrobe door trim pieces (AA) from 1 x 3 pine.

3. Cut two 66-1/4"-long side wardrobe door trim pieces (BB) from 1 x 3 pine.

4. Using *Figure 14* as a guide, arrange the four trim pieces (AA and BB) on a level surface. Center the door front (Z) over the trim pieces, leaving a 1-1/4" border of trim visible on each side of the wardrobe door front and a 1-1/8" border of trim visible at the top and bottom of the door front. Glue the pieces together and secure with 3d finishing nails spaced about 4" apart.

INSTALLING THE DOORS

1. Slide the assembled drawers into their openings, placing a scrap piece of wood between the back of each one and the back of the armoire to hold the drawers flush with the front of the armoire. Use heavy-duty, double-sided tape to stick a drawer front temporarily in place on each drawer until you have both drawer fronts positioned exactly right. Then attach the fronts to the drawers by inserting three 1-1/4" screws through each drawer and into each drawer front.

2. First measuring carefully, install the hinges on the doors so that the hinges are positioned the same distance from the top and bottom of each door.

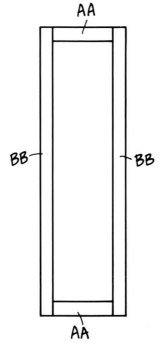

Figure 14

3. Have someone help you position the doors and attached hinges over the door openings. Line up each door so that it's even with the door and/or drawers next to it and make sure that none of the doors binds or scrapes against surrounding surfaces. When the doors are aligned, attach the hinges to the armoire.

4. Attach the drawer pulls to each of the drawers and cabinet doors, spacing them evenly and aligning them with one another.

ADDING THE TOP TRIM

1. The last step (whew!) is to add the top trim to the armoire. As you can see in the photo, we added two layers: a first layer of 1 x 4 pine and a second layer of crown molding. Be sure to take careful measurements for your trim pieces as they should be cut to fit exactly. Start by measuring and cutting two 12"-long top side trim pieces (CC) from 1 x 4 pine and one 68"-long top front trim piece (DD) from 1 x 4 pine.

2. Glue the three trim pieces (CC and DD) to the top of the armoire so that each piece overlaps the armoire by 1" and extends above it by 2-1/2". Secure the trim with 3d finishing nails spaced about 6" apart.

3. Measure and cut three pieces of crown molding to fit above the 1 x 4 pine trim, mitering the corners to fit perfectly. Glue the crown molding onto the 1 x 4 pine trim, overlapping the trim by only 1". Secure the molding to the trim with 2d finishing nails spaced about 4" apart.

FINISHING

1. Countersink all nails. Fill any nail or screw holes with wood filler.

2. Sand all surfaces thoroughly.

3. Paint or stain the completed armoire the color of your choice. We used a light green wood stain.

4. Take an admiring look at your handiwork. Then figure how to get it moved to the room where you will use it! Don't forget that it should be attached to the wall for stability.

CORNER CABINET

The cheerful cabinet shown on the next page will perk up any lonely corner in your house. The top and bottom both have storage shelves, so you can display lots of your favorite knickknacks with the doors open (or store lots of your un-favorite knickknacks with the doors closed). I used fabric in the top doors to match a bedspread, but you could substitute glass or solid panels like those in the lower doors if you like. The finished cabinet is approximately 40" wide, 78" high, and 20" deep.

The upper and lower sections of the cabinet are built separately and then joined together in the final assembly. Just take your time and follow each step carefully. This project takes a lot of work, but it's well worth it. Countersink all nails and screws as you work so that the completed project is ready for finishing.

SPECIAL TOOLS AND TECHNIQUES

Hot-glue gun

Router (optional)

Beveling

Dadoes

Mitering

Ripping

CUTTING LIST

Code	Description	Qty.	Material	Dimensions
A	Upper Floor	1	3/4" plywood	See Fig. 1 (approx. 21" x 42")
B	Upper Back	1	3/4" plywood	13-1/2" x 40"
C	Upper Side	2	3/4" plywood	17-1/2" x 40"
D	Upper Front	2	1 x 6 pine	40" long
E	Upper Shelf	2	3/4" plywood	See Fig. 5 (approx. 18" x 36")
F	Upper Top	1	3/4" plywood	Same as (E)
G	Upper Vertical Facer	2	1 x 4 pine, ripped	40" long
H	Upper Horizontal Facer	1	1 x 4 pine	25-5/8" long
I	Lower Top	1	3/4" plywood	Same as (E)
J	Lower Back	1	3/4" plywood	13-1/2" x 34-1/2"
K	Lower Side	2	3/4" plywood	17-1/2" x 34-1/2"
L	Lower Front	2	1 x 6 pine	34-1/2" long
M	Lower Shelf	1	3/4" plywood	Same as (E)
N	Lower Floor	1	3/4" plywood	Same as (E)
O	Lower Vertical Facer	2	1 x 4 pine, ripped	34-1/2" long
P	Lower Top Horizontal Facer	1	1 x 4 pine	25-5/8" long
Q	Lower Bottom Horizontal Facer	1	1 x 4 pine	25-5/8" long
R	Panel	2	1 x 12 pine	9-3/8" x 23-1/2"
S	Lower Top/ Bottom Frame	4	1 x 4 pine, ripped	8-3/4" long
T	Lower Side Frame	4	1 x 4 pine, ripped	26-7/8" long
U	Upper Top/ Bottom Frame	4	1 x 4 pine, ripped	8-3/4" long
V	Upper Side Frame	4	1 x 4 pine, ripped	36-3/8" long
W	Fabric Panel	2	fabric	23" x 33-1/2"
X	Back Reinforcement	1	2 x 2 pine	Approx. 13" long
Y	Side Reinforcement	2	2 x 2 pine	Approx. 17" long
Z	Front Reinforcement	2	2 x 2 pine	Approx. 5" long
AA	Facer Reinforcement	1	2 x 2 pine	Approx. 30" long
BB	Beaded Molding	3	3-1/2" beaded molding	Cut to fit (approx. 45" total)
CC	Fluted Molding	4	3-1/2" fluted molding	Cut to fit (approx. 142" total)
DD	Pine Trim	3	1 x 4 pine	Cut to fit (approx. 45" total)
EE	Cove Molding	3	3/4" x 3/4" cove molding	Cut to fit (approx. 45" total)
FF	Crown Molding	3	4" crown molding	Cut to fit (approx. 50" total)

Materials and Supplies

54 linear feet of 1 x 4 pine

15 linear feet of 1 x 6 pine

4 linear feet of 1 x 12 pine

8 linear feet of 2 x 2 pine

3 sheets of 3/4"-thick plywood, each 4' x 8'

4 linear feet of 3-1/2" beaded molding

4 linear feet of 3/4" x 3/4" cove molding

5 linear feet of 4" crown molding

13 linear feet of 3-1/2" fluted molding

1-1/2 yards of fabric

6 yards of upholstery braid

Hardware

Approximately 200 #6 x 1-1/4" flathead wood screws

Approximately 50 #6 x 2" flathead wood screws

Approximately 75 2d finishing nails

Approximately 200 3d finishing nails

Approximately 50 8d finishing nails

8 cabinet door hinges

4 cabinet door handles

Tacks (optional)

Notes on Materials

Because I intended to paint this cabinet, I used paint-grade 3/4"-thick plywood, and for each of the shelves, I simply filled the exposed plywood edges. If you intend to stain your cabinet, you should purchase stain-grade material. You should also buy some very thin wood veneer strips to match your plywood and glue them to the exposed edges of the cabinet shelves after they're installed.

Using careful planning, this project can be completed using 2-1/2 sheets of plywood. To accomplish this, you must cut the narrowest pieces—the upper back (B), upper sides (C), and lower back (J)—from the half-sheet. Any other combinations require you to have three full sheets.

This cabinet requires extensive beveling and mitering, so I strongly recommend that beginners who want to tackle it enlist the help of an experienced woodworker. It's not that the cuts themselves are difficult, but setting blade angles can be confusing until you know what you're doing.

Constructing the Upper Section

1. Using *Figure 1* as a guide, carefully measure and draw the outline for the upper floor (A) onto your 3/4"-thick plywood; then cut out one upper floor (A).

2. Cut one 13-1/2" x 40" upper back (B) from 3/4"-thick plywood.

3. Bevel both 40"-long edges of the upper back (B) at 22-1/2 degrees. *Figure 2* shows the angle cuts for all of the beveled edges of the upper cabinet back and sides.

4. Cut two upper sides (C) from 3/4"-thick plywood, each measuring 17-1/2" by 40".

5. Bevel one of the 40"-long edges of each upper side (C) at 22-1/2 degrees and bevel the opposite edge at 45 degrees, as shown in *Figure 2*.

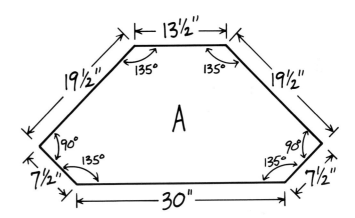

Figure 1

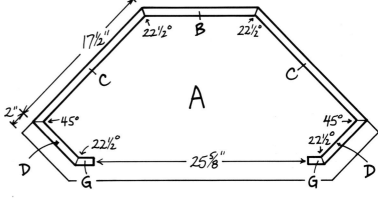

Figure 2

117

6. Cut two upper fronts (D) from 1 x 6 pine, each 40" long.

7. Bevel one of the 40"-long edges of each of the upper fronts (D) at 22-1/2 degrees. Bevel the opposite edge at 45 degrees.

8. The assembly of the upper cabinet is shown in *Figures 2* and *3*. You would probably be wise to enlist the assistance of a willing helper (or two) to accomplish this task. Study both diagrams to familiarize yourself with how the pieces go together. Assembly won't be the best of times to have to say, "Hand me that book again—how does it fit together?"

As shown in *Figures 2* and *3*, the upper back (B), upper sides (C) and upper fronts (D) stand on end on top of the upper floor

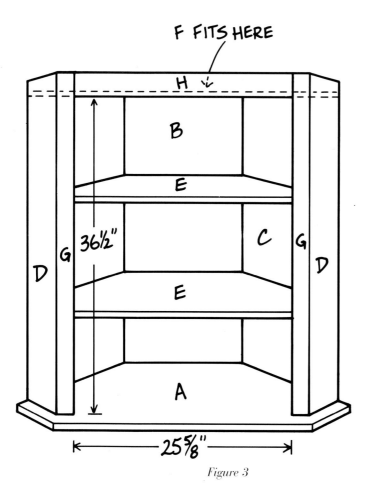

Figure 3

(A). The upper back (B) is set flush with the 13-1/2" edge of the upper floor (A), with its narrower face on the inside of the cabinet. The upper sides (C) are flush with the 19-1/2" edges of the upper floor, and their 22-1/2-degree beveled edges fit against the matching beveled edges of the upper back (B). Notice, however, that the 17-1/2"-long end of each upper side (C) is 2" shorter than the corresponding 19-1/2" edge of the upper floor (A). The excess width of the upper floor (A) creates a small "shelf" between the upper and lower cabinet assemblies (see *Figure 3*). This becomes an important design element in the finished project.

Begin by attaching the upper back (B) to the upper floor (A). Glue the parts together and insert 1-1/4" screws through the bottom of the upper floor (A) and into the edge of the upper back (B), spacing the screws about 3" apart.

9. Fit the 22-1/2-degree beveled edge of one upper side (C) against the matching beveled edge of the upper back (B), positioning the side (C) so that its outer face is flush with the edge of the upper floor (A). Glue the parts together and insert 1-1/4" screws through the upper floor (A) and into the edge of the upper side (C), spacing the screws about 3" apart. Then insert 3d finishing nails through the bevel in the upper back (B) and into the beveled edge of the upper side (C), spacing the nails about 4" apart.

10. Repeat Step 9 to attach the remaining upper side (C) to the upper floor (A) and the upper back (B).

11. The next step is to add the two fronts (D), using *Figure 2* as a guide. Note that the 45-degree beveled edge of each front (D) fits against the matching bevel on the adjacent upper side (C). Glue the parts together and insert 1-1/4" screws through the upper floor (A) into the edges of the upper fronts (D), spacing the screws about 3" apart. Secure the bevels with 3d finishing nails spaced about 4" apart.

ADDING THE SHELVES AND TOP

1. *Figure 4* shows the dimensions of the two upper shelves (E) and the top (F). The shelves must fit exactly inside the assembly. To assure a good fit, first cut a cardboard pattern of an upper shelf (E), using the dimensions provided in *Figure 4*. Position the cardboard pattern inside your assembly, check the fit, and alter the pattern as necessary. Then use the altered pattern to trace two upper shelves (E) and one upper top (F) onto 3/4"-thick plywood, and cut out the plywood parts.

2. Place the assembly right side up on a level surface and decide where to place the shelves. I positioned the first shelf 12" above the floor and the second shelf 12" above that, but you may space the shelves as you like. Next, measure and mark both the upper back (B) and upper sides (C) with the desired locations of the shelves. The marks don't have to be exact—your job will be much easier if you use a level to position the shelves rather than relying on measurements.

3. Fit the lowest upper shelf (E) inside the cabinet assembly as close as possible to your marks. Place the level on the upper shelf (E) in several locations and facing in several directions, adjusting the position of the shelf until it is exactly level in every direction.

4. Use glue and 1-1/4" screws placed about 3" apart to attach the shelf in place. Insert the screws through the upper sides (C), the upper back (B), and the upper fronts (D) into the upper shelf (E), countersinking each screw as you go.

5. Repeat Steps 3 and 4 to attach the second upper shelf (E) inside the upper cabinet assembly.

6. Fit the upper top (F) inside the upper cabinet assembly as you did when adding the shelves, positioning its lower face 3-1/2" from the top edges of the upper back, sides, and fronts (B, C, and D). Use your level again to make sure that the top (F) is even in all directions.

7. Glue the upper top (F) in place and insert 1-1/4" screws, spaced about 3"

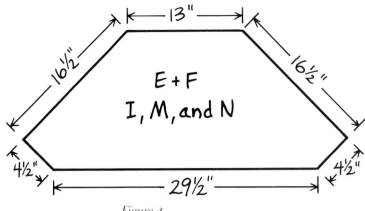

Figure 4

apart, through the upper sides (C), the upper back (B), and both upper fronts (D) into the upper top (F).

INSTALLING THE FACERS

1. Cut two 40"-long upper vertical facers (G) from 1 x 4 pine.

2. Rip each of the upper vertical facers (G) to 2-1/4" in width.

3. Bevel one 40"-long edge of each upper vertical facer (G) at 22-1/2 degrees, as shown in *Figure 2*.

4. To avoid later problems with the doors, perform this next step without using any glue. Using *Figures 2* and *3* as guides, attach one upper vertical facer (G) to the left upper front (D), the two upper shelves (E), and the upper top (F). Note that the 22-1/2-degree bevels on the upper vertical facer (G) and the upper front (D) face each other. Secure the meeting beveled edges of the upper front (D) and the upper vertical facer (G) by driving two 3d finishing nails just far enough in to hold the piece in place.

5. Repeat Step 4 to attach the remaining upper vertical facer (G) to the right-hand side of the cabinet assembly, again omitting the glue.

6. Check the width of the opening between the two upper vertical facers (G) along the exposed edge of the top (F). Also measure the width of the opening across the middle and bottom. The opening should measure exactly 25-5/8", or the doors will not fit properly. To adjust the opening, remove the two upper vertical facers (G) and alter them as necessary. Then glue the adjusted facers in place and insert 1-1/4" screws through the upper floor (A) and into the bottom edges of the upper vertical facers (G). Secure the meeting beveled edges of the upper front (D) and the upper vertical facer (G) with 3d finishing nails spaced about 6" apart. Also drive nails through the facers (G) and into the edges of the shelves (E) and the upper top (F).

7. Cut one 25-5/8"-long upper horizontal facer (H) from 1 x 4 pine.

8. Fit the upper horizontal facer (H) between the two upper vertical facers (G) and position it so that its bottom edge is flush with the lower face of the upper top (F). Drive two 3d finishing nails through the upper horizontal facer (H) into the edge of the upper top (F), hammering them in only far enough to hold the piece in place.

9. Now measure the opening from top to bottom on the left and right sides and in the middle. It should measure exactly 36-1/2", as shown in *Figure 3*. If necessary, remove the upper horizontal facer (H) and alter it so that the opening conforms to these measurements.

10. Replace the upper horizontal facer (H), glue it in place, and secure with 3d finishing nails placed about 3" apart and driven into the edge of the upper top (F). Also toe-nail through the ends of the upper horizontal facer (H) into each of the upper vertical facers (G).

CONSTRUCTING THE LOWER SECTION

1. The construction of the lower section is very similar to that of the upper section. There are several exceptions in the measurements of the parts and in the assembly process, however, so follow the directions carefully.

The lower top (I) has exactly the same dimensions as the upper shelves (E). Use your cardboard pattern again to cut one lower top (I) from 3/4"-thick plywood.

2. Cut one 13-1/2" x 34-1/2" lower back (J) from 3/4"-thick plywood.

3. Bevel each of the 34-1/2"-long sides of the lower back (J) at 22-1/2 degrees, as shown in *Figure 5*.

4. Cut two lower sides (K) from 3/4"-thick plywood, each measuring 17-1/2" x 34-1/2".

5. Bevel one 34-1/2" edge of each lower side (K) at 22-1/2 degrees. Bevel the opposite edge at a 45-degree angle (see *Figure 5*).

6. Cut two 34-1/2"-long lower fronts (L) from 1 x 6 pine.

7. Bevel one of the 34-1/2"-long edges of each of the lower fronts (L) at a 45-degree angle. Bevel the opposite edge at 22-1/2 degrees.

8. The assembly of the lower cabinet is shown in *Figures 5* and *6*. Again, enlist the services of a helper and study the diagrams before beginning the assembly.

For ease of handling, the lower cabinet is assembled upside down, with the lower top (I) serving as a base. Note that the lower back (J) and lower sides (K) fit onto the edges of the lower top (I), not on its face. Make sure that the narrower faces of the beveled lower back (J) and lower sides (K) are on the inside of the cabinet and that the 22-1/2-degree bevels are matched together.

9. Begin by gluing the lower back (J) to the lower top (I). Insert 1-1/4" screws, spaced about 3" apart, through the lower back (J) and into the edge of the lower top (I).

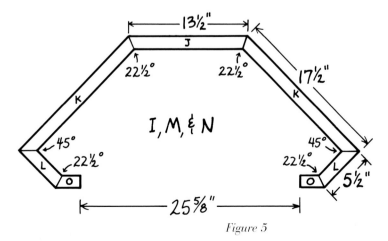

Figure 5

10. Glue one lower side (K) to the lower top (I) and lower back (J), matching the 22-1/2-degree bevels. Insert 3d finishing nails, spaced about 4" apart, through the lower back (J) and into the beveled edge of the lower side (K). Insert 1-1/4" screws, spaced about 3" apart, through the lower side (K) and into the edge of the lower top (I).

11. Repeat Step 10 to attach the remaining lower side (K) to the lower top (I) and the lower back (J).

12. The next step is to add the two lower fronts (L), using *Figures 5 and 6* as assembly guides. Note that the 45-degree beveled edges of the lower fronts (L) and the lower sides (K) fit together. Glue the lower fronts (L) in place and insert 3d finishing nails spaced about 3" apart through their beveled edges and into the beveled edges of the lower sides (K). Also insert 1-1/4" screws through the lower fronts (L) into the edge of the lower top (I).

ADDING THE SHELF AND FLOOR

1. The lower shelf (M) and the lower floor (N) are the same dimensions as the lower top (I). Use your cardboard pattern again to cut one lower shelf (M) and one lower floor (N) from 3/4"-thick plywood.

2. Place the lower cabinet assembly upside down on a surface that is exactly level. Position the lower shelf (M) inside it as you like. I positioned mine 13" from the lower top (I). Measure and mark both the lower back (J) and the two lower sides (K) with the desired shelf location.

3. Fit the lower shelf (M) inside the lower cabinet assembly as close as possible to your marks. Use your level to make sure that the lower shelf (M) is exactly level in all directions.

4. Glue the shelf in place and insert 1-1/4" screws, spaced about 3" apart, through the lower sides (K), the lower back (J), and the lower fronts (L) into the edges of the lower shelf (M).

5. Fit the lower floor (N) inside the lower cabinet assembly as you did with the shelf (M), positioning what will be its upper face (when the cabinet is turned right side up)

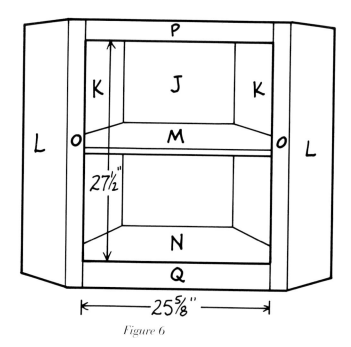

Figure 6

3-1/2" from the exposed edges of the lower back, lower sides, and lower fronts (J, K, and L). Again, level the lower floor (N) in all directions.

6. Glue the lower floor in place and insert 1-1/4" screws, spaced about 3" apart, through the lower fronts (L), the lower sides (K) and the lower back (J) into the lower floor (N).

ADDING THE FACERS

1. Turn the lower cabinet assembly right side up. Cut two lower vertical facers (O) from 1 x 4 pine, each 34-1/2" long.

2. Rip each of the lower vertical facers (O) to 2-1/4" in width.

3. Bevel one 34-1/2"-long edge of each lower vertical facer (O) at 22-1/2 degrees.

4. Note in *Figure 5* that the beveled edge of the lower vertical facer matches the beveled edge of the lower front (L). Attach one lower vertical facer (O) to the left lower front (L), the lower shelf (M), and the lower top (I), as shown in *Figure 6*, using two 3d finishing nails driven in just far enough to hold the piece in place.

5. Repeat Step 4 to attach the remaining lower vertical facer (O) to the other side of the cabinet assembly.

¼" × ⅜" DADO

Figure 7

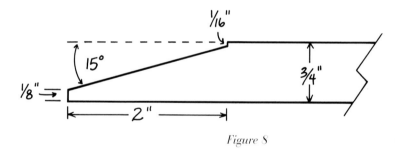

Figure 8

6. Check the width of the opening between the two lower vertical facers (O) along the exposed edge of the lower floor (N), across the center of the opening, and across the top. The opening should measure exactly 25-5/8". If necessary, remove the two lower vertical facers (O) and alter them to make the opening conform to this measurement. Then glue the two lower vertical facers (O) in place and drive 3d finishing nails, spaced about 4" apart, through the beveled edges of the lower fronts (L) into the edges of the lower vertical facers (O). Also insert 1-1/4" screws through the facers (O) into the edges of the lower floor (N) and lower shelf (M).

7. From 1 x 4 pine, cut one 25-5/8"-long lower top horizontal facer (P) and one 25-5/8"-long lower bottom horizontal facer (Q).

8. Fit the lower bottom horizontal facer (Q) between the two lower vertical facers (O), positioning it so that its top edge is flush with the upper surface of the lower floor (N). Glue the facer (Q) in place and secure it with 3d finishing nails driven through the facer (Q) and into the edge of the floor (N). Also toenail the ends of the facer (Q) to the edges of the lower vertical facers (O).

9. Fit the lower top horizontal facer (P) between the two lower vertical facers (O) so that it is flush at the top. Secure it temporarily by driving two 3d finishing nails through the facer (P) and into the edge of the lower top (I). Hammer the nails in only far enough to hold the piece in place.

10. Now measure the opening from top to bottom on the left, middle, and right sides. The opening should measure exactly 27-1/2". If necessary, remove the lower top horizontal facer (P) and alter it so that the opening conforms to this measurement.

11. Glue the lower top horizontal facer (P) in place, securing it by driving 3d finishing nails through it and into the edge of the lower top (I). Space the nails about 3" apart. Also toenail the facer by driving nails through its edge and into the lower vertical facers (O).

Constructing the Lower Doors

1. Each of the two lower doors (see *Figure 7*) consists of a center panel that is beveled on all four edges and inserted into a frame. This is not difficult to do, but it requires a certain amount of precision in cutting to obtain a professional-looking finished product. Don't hurry the process; be meticulous in your work.

Start by cutting one 9-3/8" by 23-1/2" panel (R) from 1 x 12 pine.

2. Set your saw blade to cut at 15 degrees off vertical and bevel all four edges of the panel (R), leaving a thickness of 1/8" on the outside edges. A diagram of the resulting cut is shown in *Figure 8*.

3. Rip a total of 12 linear feet of 1 x 4 pine to 2" in width.

4. From the ripped 1 x 4 pine, cut two 8-3/4"-long lower top/bottom frame pieces (S) and two 26-7/8"-long lower side frame pieces (T).

5. Cut a dado 1/4" wide and 3/8" deep down the center inside edge of each of the four frame pieces (S and T) to accommodate the center panel (R). If you don't want your dadoes to show (what would the neighbors think?) on the outer edges of the doors, then start the dado 1" from one end of each lower side frame piece (T) and stop it 1" from the other end.

6. Place the panel (R) into the dadoes cut in the frame pieces to make sure that all of the pieces fit together properly. An optional step at this point is to rout a decorative design into the inside edges of the frame pieces. Because this is difficult to do with the panel installed, simply clamp the frame together securely and rout the inside edges. Then place the panel (R) inside the frame.

7. As shown in *Figure 7*, the top and bottom frame pieces (S) fit between the side frame pieces (T). Glue and clamp the frame pieces together, with the panel (R) in place but not glued into the dadoes. Fasten the frame together by inserting 8d finishing nails at all four corners.

8. Repeat Steps 1 through 7 to assemble the second lower door.

Constructing the Upper Door Frames

1. The upper doors are constructed in the same manner as the lower doors, but they don't have raised panels in their centers. Instead, the upper doors are completed by adding fabric after the cabinet has been stained or painted. Start by ripping a total of 16 linear feet of 1 x 4 to 2" in width.

2. From the ripped pine, cut two 8-3/4"-long upper top/bottom frame pieces, (U) and two 36-3/8"-long upper side frame pieces (V).

3. Glue and clamp the four frame pieces (U and V) together as shown in *Figure 7*,

making sure to fit the upper top/bottom frame pieces (U) between the upper side frame pieces (V). Then drive 8d finishing nails into all four corners of the frame.

If you routed a decorative design onto the lower doors, you may want to rout one into the inside edges of the assembled frame at this stage.

4. Repeat Steps 1 through 3 to make the second upper door frame.

Hanging the Doors

1. Set the cabinet assemblies on their backs so that you don't have to support the weight of the doors while you hang them.

2. Set both of the upper doors inside the opening in the upper cabinet assembly. If you're using exposed hinges, position them equidistant from the top and bottom on the outside of each door and secure them in place using the screws provided by the manufacturer. For other kinds of hinges, follow the manufacturer's instructions for installation.

3. Repeat Step 2 to attach the two lower doors to the lower cabinet assembly.

4. Attach the four cabinet handles (one on each door), following the manufacturer's directions.

Completing the Base

1. The lower back (J), lower sides (K), lower fronts (L), and lower vertical and horizontal facers (O, P, and Q) form a 3-1/2"-wide collar at the bottom of the lower cabinet. In order to support the weight of the cabinet, this collar must be strengthened with 2 x 2 pine reinforcements.

Cut the following pieces from 2 x 2 pine:

Code	Description	Qty.	Length
X	Back Reinforcement	1	13"
Y	Side Reinforcement	2	17"
Z	Front Reinforcement	2	5"
AA	Facer Reinforcement	1	30"

As you can see in *Figure 9*, the reinforcements must be mitered to fit the beveled edges of the pieces they reinforce. The lengths specified above give you some excess for mitering room. Measure and miter carefully so that all of the reinforcements fit properly.

2. Start by mitering both ends of the back reinforcement (X) at 22-1/2 degrees, as shown in *Figure 9*.

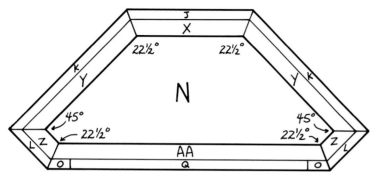

Figure 9

3. Then miter each of the side reinforcements (Y) and front reinforcements (Z) to create a 22-1/2-degree cut at one end and a 45-degree cut at the other end.

4. Finally, miter both ends of the facer reinforcement (AA) at 22-1/2 degrees.

5. Fit the back reinforcement (X) against the lower back (J) and under and against the lower floor (N). Glue it in place and insert 2" screws, placed about 3" apart, through the back reinforcement and into the floor (N) and lower back (J).

6. Fit the two side reinforcements (Y) in place, matching the miters as you do. Glue them to the lower sides (K) and lower floor (N) and insert screws as in Step 5.

7. Fit the two front reinforcements (Z) in place, again matching the miters. Glue them to the lower fronts (L) and lower floor (N) and insert screws as in Step 5.

8. Fit the facer reinforcement (AA) in place. Glue it to both vertical facers (O), the lower bottom horizontal facer (Q), and the lower floor (N). Then insert screws as in Step 5.

ASSEMBLING THE CABINET

1. Place the upper cabinet assembly on top of the lower cabinet assembly, matching the upper and lower assemblies at the back and on the sides.

2. If you want to be able to separate the two assemblies (during a household move, for example), use only screws—not glue—so that you can unscrew the two halves for easier moving. Insert 1-1/4" screws through the lower top (I) into the upper floor (A). (You can reverse the direction of the screws, but the heads will be visible unless you countersink and fill them, making this a permanent attachment.) Use two or three screws across the back, two or three in the middle, and three or four across the front.

ADDING THE TRIM

1. Study *Figure 10*, which shows the pine trim (DD), cove molding (EE), and crown molding (FF) added to the cabinet top; the fluted trim (CC) added to both sides; and beaded molding (BB) added to the bottom. Because the back and sides of the cabinet fit against the wall, no molding is added to them.

2. Carefully measure and cut two 6-1/2"-long pieces of beaded molding (BB) to fit across the lower fronts (L) at the bottom of the cabinet and one 32"-long piece to fit across the lower facers (O and Q). Miter one end of each shorter piece and both ends of the longer piece at 22-1/2 degrees. Glue the mitered pieces of beaded molding (BB) to the cabinet and secure with 3d finishing nails spaced about 3" apart.

3. Measure and cut two pieces of fluted molding (CC) to fit down the center of each of the lower fronts (L), between the upper floor (A) and the beaded molding (BB) that you just installed. Each piece should be approximately 31" long. Glue the pieces in place and secure with 2d finishing nails spaced about 4" apart. (Don't glue the end of the fluted molding (CC) to the upper floor (A) if you plan to separate the upper and lower assemblies at some future time.)

4. Measure the length of each upper front (D) along its center, starting at the upper floor (A) and extending 2-1/2" higher than the top of the opening for the upper doors. This length should be approximately 39". Cut two pieces of fluted molding (CC) to this length. Glue the pieces in place and secure with 2d finishing nails spaced about 4" apart.

5. Following the same procedures described in Step 2, measure, cut, and miter 1 x 4 pine trim (DD) to fit around the top of the cabinet. The lower edges of the shorter trim pieces (DD) fit on top of the fluted molding (CC) that you attached in Step 4. Note that the pine trim (DD) will extend above the upper surface of the cabinet. Glue the trim in place and secure with 1-1/4" countersunk screws.

6. Again following the same procedures, measure, cut, and miter 3/4" x 3/4" cove molding (EE) to fit across the top of the cabinet. Use glue and 3d finishing nails to attach the cove molding just below the 1 x 4 pine trim (DD) that you added in Step 5. The ends of the cove molding (EE) stop at the edges of the fluted molding (CC).

7. The final addition is the crown molding (FF) that fits across the very top of the cabinet. Following the procedures in Step 5, attach the crown molding (FF) so that it overlaps the top of the 1 x 4 pine trim (DD) by 1".

FINISHING THE WOOD

1. Fill all nail and screw holes with wood filler. If you want to be able to disassemble the cabinet for transport, don't cover the screw holes in the lower top (I), as these screws hold the two assemblies together.

2. Sand all the surfaces thoroughly.

3. Check the fit of each pair of doors. If they bind or scrape the edges of the opening, sand or plane them as necessary.

4. Stain or paint the cabinet and all four doors the color of your choice.

ADDING THE FABRIC

1. Cut two 23" x 33-1/2" fabric panels (W) for the upper doors.

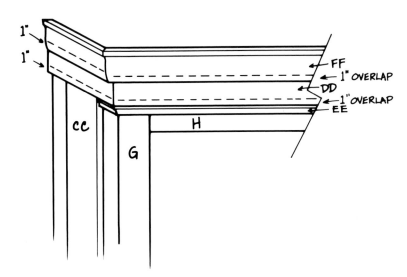

Figure 10

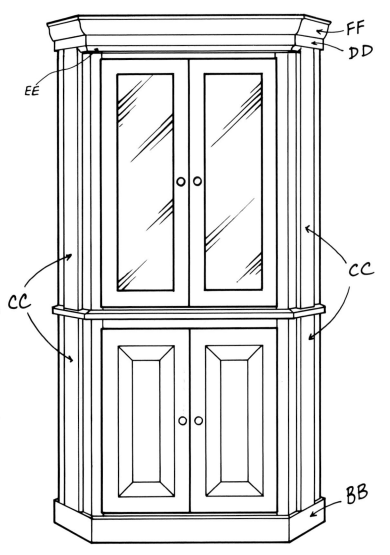

2. Sew gathering stitches 1/4" from the edge along both 23"-long edges of one fabric panel.

3. Pull the gathering stitches until the panel measures 11-3/4" across the top and bottom.

4. Hot-glue or tack the gathered panel to the inside of one upper cabinet door. Trim the gathered edges with scissors, then glue upholstery braid around all four edges of the gathered panel to conceal the gathering stitches.

5. Repeat Steps 2 through 4 to stitch and attach a fabric panel to the inside of the remaining upper door.

6. Now sit down, lean back, and admire your work!

METRIC CONVERSION CHARTS

Inches	CM		Inches	CM
1/8	0.3		24	61.0
1/4	0.6		25	63.5
3/8	1.0		26	66.0
1/2	1.3		27	68.6
5/8	1.6		28	71.1
3/4	1.9		29	73.7
7/8	2.2		30	76.2
1	2.5		31	78.7
1-1/4	3.2		32	81.3
1-1/2	3.8		33	83.8
1-3/4	4.4		34	86.4
2	5.1		35	88.9
2-1/2	6.4		36	91.4
3	7.6		37	94.0
3-1/2	8.9		38	96.5
4	10.2		39	99.1
4-1/2	11.4		40	101.6
5	12.7		41	104.1
6	15.2		42	106.7
7	17.8		43	109.2
8	20.3		44	111.8
9	22.9		45	114.3
10	25.4		46	116.8
11	27.9		47	119.4
12	30.5		48	121.9
13	33.0		49	124.5
14	35.6		50	127.0
15	38.1			
16	40.6			
17	43.2			
18	45.7			
19	48.3			
20	50.8			
21	53.3			
22	55.9			
23	58.4			

Volumes

1 fluid ounce	29.6 ml
1 pint	473 ml
1 quart	946 ml
1 gallon (128 fl. oz.)	3.785 l

Weights

0.035 ounces	1 gram
1 ounce	28.35 grams
1 pound	453.6 grams

ACKNOWLEDGEMENTS

If this book is successful, much of the credit will belong to people other than this author. Many thanks to:

Mark Baldwin (Bradenton, FL), who shared equally in the design and production of all the projects in this book, who cheerfully took on the heavy stuff, and who always came up with brilliant solutions to difficult problems. He's a wonder!

Chris Rich (Altamont Press, Asheville, NC), my editor and friend, who spent hundreds of hours checking and rechecking me and who exhibited patience throughout the preparation of this manuscript. Cheers, Chris!

Evan Bracken (Light Reflections, Hendersonville, NC) and Leslie Dierks (Altamont Press, Asheville, NC), who "shot till they dropped" during our marathon photo shoot. You made a huge chore enjoyable.

Kathy Holmes and **Elaine Thompson** (art director and typesetter at Altamont Press, Asheville, NC), for their inspired and careful work

Orrin Lundgren (Asheville, NC), for his illustrations

Rob Pulleyn (Altamont Press, Asheville, NC), world's finest publisher, for his professional and personal support

Patti Kertz (Longboat Key, FL) and **Craig Weiss** (Asheville, NC), for their generous help with photography

INDEX